TIBETAN DIARY

By the same author:

China Diary After Mao
China Diary
Russian Diary
Asian Diary
Mountaintop Kingdom: Sikkim, with *Alice Kandell*

Tibetan Diary
Charlotte Y. Salisbury

WALKER AND COMPANY
NEW YORK

For my daughter Charlotte,
with boundless love and admiration

Salisbury, Charlotte Y.
  Tibetan diary, and travels along the old silk route.

    1. Tibet (China) —Description and travel. 2. Silk Road—Description and travel. 3. Salisbury, Charlotte Y. I. Title.
DS786.S284   1981   915.1'50458   80–54816
ISBN 0–8027–0683–6   AACR2

First published in the United States of America in 1981 by the Walker Publishing Company, Inc.

Published simultaneously in Canada by John Wiley & Sons Canada, Limited, Rexdale, Ontario

ISBN: 0-8027-0683-5

Library of Congress Catalog Card Number: 80-54816

Printed in the United States of America

10 9 8 7 6 5 4 3 2 1

Introduction

In 1966, when Americans were not permitted to go to China, my husband, Harrison Salisbury, an editor of *The New York Times*, and I made a 40,000 mile trip around the periphery of that country. We started in Hong Kong where we talked to many China watchers, the title given to our diplomats and journalists whose frustrating profession was to sit on the border watching and listening for any trickle of information from inside China. We met with their English counterparts, as well as with businessmen from all over. We dined with a Chinese friend of many years who lives abroad. He wanted to introduce us to some mainland Chinese, but they refused to meet us. Americans were the number one enemies.

From Hong Kong we went to Cambodia, where Americans had had no contact since we closed our embassy in 1965. Here again we talked to Asian and European diplomats and journalists and almost everyone in the Cambodian government.

In Burma we dined alone with General Ne Win and his wife and met the few foreigners who had not been expelled, always seeking information about China and some way of breaking down the barriers.

Then to India and up to Sikkim, which was an independent country at that time, caught between the two giants, China and India. We traveled to Moscow, to Outer Mongolia, across Siberia and to Japan by boat. At every point Harrison hoped a miracle would occur and we would be allowed to cross the border into the forbidden land. But it never happened.

In 1970 I flew to Sikkim and spent a month in that tiny country gathering material for a book. The Sikkimese people were having a hard time because the border to Tibet had been closed. Though Sikkim was in some ways independent, and was labeled independent, India exercised political control, was responsible for Sikkim's defense and regarded Sikkim's border with Tibet as the Indian border with China.

Prior to the border closing, the Sikkimese and Tibetans had many ties. They are the same kind of people, families were related, some living in Sikkim, some in Tibet. The Sikkimese drove their sheep and yak across the border to the fertile Chumbi valley in Tibet, and pastured them there every summer. Trade flourished between the two countries and they shared the same special Tibetan brand of Buddhism.

All this intermingling ceased and today Indian and Chinese armies face each other on the northern border of Sikkim, seized by India and now proclaimed an Indian state.

In 1972, soon after Nixon's famous visit, the way at last was open and Harrison and I made our first trip to mainland China. That year we traveled from Beijing to Xi'an, to Yan'an where the Long March ended, to Changsha, near where Chairman Mao was born. We stayed in Wuhan, a huge industrial city, called one of the three "ovens" of China, it is so hot. The Cultural Revolution had simmered down momentarily and Zhou

Enlai was pretty much in charge in Beijing. We dined with him at the Great Hall of the People, we had interviews with other diplomats, Chinese and foreign. After so many years of seeing nothing and having to rely on other peoples' views, what we saw and heard was exciting. The spirit seemed fresh, China seemed united, the people working with one idea in mind—to build up their country.

In 1977 we went again. There were many changes. Zhou Enlai was dead. He had been reviled by the Gang of Four in his last days. Chairman Mao had died several months later. The Gang of Four had been arrested one month after that. Hua Guofeng was chairman and titular head of the government, though Deng Hsaio-ping, a vice chairman, was running things. This time we traveled to northeast China, to Harbin, to the great oilfields of Taching, to Huhehot and Silinhot in Inner Mongolia. Again to Shanghai, to Hangzhou and Guangzhou (Canton). This time we began to hear details of what went on during the Cultural Revolution, the damage to industry, science, education, medicine. Everyone said "We have lost ten years."

On both those trips we asked to go to Tibet, but the answers were always the same. "Not at this time." "The Cultural Revolution is still going on there." "There are not proper facilities." "It is too hot." "Too cold." "Too high." "You are too old." I gave up hope of ever getting there, to the land of our dreams.

The trip I describe in this book is our third, and longest trip to China, taken in the summer of 1980. This time we followed the old Silk Road from Lanzhou to Dunhuang where we saw the Buddhist caves. To Turpan, Ürümqi and Ili, not far from the Soviet border. We went again to

Xi'an, primarily to see the now famous clay figures that were discovered in 1974 by peasants digging for an irrigation project. We went to Chengdu and finally, after days of being told first yes, then no, after all those years of longing, we flew to the place we had wanted to see more than any in the world—Tibet.

Modern Chinese Transliteration

Old Spellings (Wade-Giles)	New Spellings (Pinyin)
Canton	Guangzhou
Chengtu	Chengdu
Chingkang Mountains	Jinggan Shan
Hangchow	Hangzhou
Huhehot	Hohhot
Lanchow	Lanzhou
Peking	Beijing
Sian	Xi'an
Turfan	Turpan
Ürümchi	Ürümqi
Kansu Province	Gansu Sheng
Kaolan Mountains	Gaolan Sheng
Yellow River	Huang He

Sunday, July 20, 1980
at the Kowloon Station, Hong Kong

AS I SIT in this spic-and-span train starting off from the big, new railway station, it is hard to equate this trip to China with the one I took eight years ago. The only thing the same is the temperature outside: boiling hot and humid.

At that time I got aboard a dirty train that left from the filthy old Hong Kong Station. The Chinese passengers were just local people going to the little towns on this side of the border at Shumchun, where they lived and worked. There were only a few other people, mostly diplomats, including the ambassador to China from Peru and his wife and daughter. I sat with them on the train and walked across the now famous railroad bridge between Lo Wu, on the Hong Kong side, and Shumchun, in mainland China. There were no through trains then. Trains stopped on either side of the bridge, passengers got out, carried their bags across, and went through customs on the other side. I lunched in the clean and airy dining room in the Chinese station before boarding the spotless train to Guangzhou. There I was met by a lovely young Chinese man who took me to the airport and saw me on the plane to Beijing.

Today's train, starting at Hong Kong, goes straight through to Guangzhou. No changing trains at the border.

No walking across the bridge. This train is clean, it has slipcovers and antimacassars on the chairs and lace curtains at the windows. And—something I have never encountered before on a Chinese train—it is air-conditioned.

Most of today's passengers are Chinese. Many have American or other foreign passports. They look prosperous, excited, and happy, and they are laden down with more stuff than I have ever seen any people travel with. Tape recorders, TV sets, radios, electric irons—and it is obvious from the boxes they are packed in that they have never been opened. Everything is brand-new. Heaven knows what more is in the huge bags and suitcases that fill the overhead racks and crowd the floor, even the aisles. The woman opposite me is sitting next to the window; there are boxes on the seat between her and her companion; boxes piled on the floor in front of them so that they have no room for their legs, which are stretched out on top of the baggage; boxes and bags on their laps.

These are overseas Chinese. (*Overseas Chinese* is the name by which Chinese born abroad are called. They are always Chinese, whether they are citizens of another country or not.) They are going to China to see their families. I have never met an overseas Chinese who did not have a sizable number of relatives living in China. Many have not seen them since 1949, the time of the Communist Liberation. No wonder they look excited. I would like to see the looks on the relatives' faces when they see all the remarkable things being brought to them.

From a TV screen over the door a pretty woman is speaking, first in Chinese, then in English, saying "Welcome aboard" and explaining about the train. There is a diner serving both Western and Chinese food, toilets at each end of the car, and so on. Now a young man in a Western suit is looking out from the screen and singing in praise of some scenery. He looks more like a Japanese TV star or movie actor than a product of the People's Republic of China. Next another pretty woman, in a long dress, earrings, and fashionable hairdo, is singing. The climax, as I am writing this, is a Japanese-looking young man singing "Eidelweiss" in Chinese.

En route

LOOKING OUT the window, I see changes, too. There isn't as much trash and litter on the Hong Kong side as I remember. Also there is an enormous amount of building being done on both sides of the border. As we are going through the lush rice fields after crossing the bridge, I see one piece of farm machinery, a walking tractor. That's more than we have seen in this area before.

At the Guangzhou Airport, 6:15 P.M.

WE WERE MET by Mr. Whu, of the Travel Service. We had no plane tickets to Beijing, but Mr. Whu was able to obtain some, and he accompanied us here. We have checked our bags and Mr. Whu has left. We will fly to Beijing in about an hour, and Harrison is afraid we will not be met at the airport. He was not able to call the Foreign Office and doesn't know if Mr. Whu will. Not a very pleasant prospect: no bed, no dinner. Well, we'll see.

We are sitting in the regular waiting room of this airport, not in the special room for foreigners, though there is one right next to this, screened off and empty. On our two previous trips to this country we never sat in the Chinese waiting rooms; we were always hustled into the special places for visitors. Today we are just ordinary travelers; it's very nice.

Most of the people waiting here are Chinese, and everyone seems to be drinking Coca-Cola, which can be bought in bottles from a machine. The women and girls are wearing bright-colored blouses, and many have skirts. Their sandals are pink, blue, gold. There are ads everywhere, for travel agents and companies in Hong Kong, even some for cosmetics. And in billboard space where there is no ad, signs advertise: "Space available for ad—contact agency in Hong Kong." How very different! Even three years ago there were no ads, never anything but revolutionary posters urging people to unite, to work hard, to build up the country. And very few women wore colors, only the regulation blue or gray pants and shirt. Also, there are a few flies, and though we did see a few in 1977, in 1972 there were practically none. If one did appear, it caused a crisis.

But one thing that is the same is the lost-and-found department. Behind a glass window is a collection of objects picked up in the airport. Umbrellas, fans, change purses, sweaters, magazines—all carefully labeled with the date each item was found. Included is a string bag of apples, all withered and brown, but still waiting to be claimed. I remember that I left a small pillow in the hotel in Guangzhou on our way home during our last trip. I wrote the hotel from Hong Kong and told them what room we had had, and soon after we got home to New York, my pillow arrived, wrapped up in a cloth cover and sent by air. So this kind of honesty doesn't seem to have changed.

Monday, July 21, 9:30 A.M.
At the Airport Hotel in Beijing

BEFORE 1978 most English-speaking people used the
Wade-Giles system of transliterating Chinese into
English, which was invented by an Englishman. With
the normalization of relations between the United States
and China, it was decided in the United States to replace
the Wade-Giles system with that of Pinyin, invented by
the Chinese themselves. This system is more accurate in
its sounds. For example, Beijing actually sounds more like
the way the Chinese pronounce the name of their capital.
But all names and words are different, and I don't know
all the Pinyin, so this diary will be quite a hodgepodge of
transliteration, or else all the old and I'll change it when I
get home.

After an hour's wait in the Guangzhou airport we got
on the plane that brought us here. The first thing I
noticed was the stewardesses in bright blue skirts and
jackets and white shirts—a uniform similar to that worn
by stewardesses all over the world, not the baggy khaki
pants we saw on earlier trips. We had seats assigned, and
as soon as we were airborne, we were given little cups of
sherbet, something I remember from flights to and from
Shanghai. A "little snack" followed, consisting of cold
chicken, sausage, bread, bamboo shoots, a few pastry
things, cake, and tea. Very good. When we first took off,
one of the stewardesses went through the plane with a fly
swatter, killing groggy flies on the ceiling and very
carefully putting them, without touching them, on a
piece of paper.

So, the flight was nice, and I slept most of the four
hours. When we arrived, as H. had feared, there was no

5

one from the Foreign Office nor any real guide for us. But Mr. Whu in Guangzhou had telephoned ahead, and a pleasant young man from the Travel Service met us and put us in a taxi that took us here. We decided to stay in this hotel for the night rather than go in to Beijing. Like all airport hotels, it is practically on the airfield, it is new, clean, and modern. We were very comfortable in a big double bed that nearly filled the room. (It also turned out to be terribly expensive, about $55 in American dollars, compared with our room at the Beijing Hotel, which was $30.) Harrison called the Foreign Office and got Yao Wei. (He was our guide and interpreter in 1972 and is now in the Foreign Office.) He felt badly about our not being met, but H. said it was all our own fault. We should have wired or telephoned from Hong Kong.

So we have had an awfully good breakfast in the dining room: that wonderful toast and delicious strawberry jam. H. had ham and eggs, and I had a single boiled egg. I forgot that they are hard-boiled unless we ask for it soft, and the waitress thought I was nutty when I asked for a spoon. I was supposed to peel it, which I did. Now we are waiting to be picked up and taken to the hotel where we'll be staying while we're in Beijing.

The bathroom has been cleaned very nicely. The tiles were put in well, and it all looks more like a hotel bathroom in the United States or Europe than any did on our previous visits.

Later at the Beijing Hotel, 6:00 P.M.

YAO WEI came out to see us at the Airport Hotel—so nice of him. He brought with him Tu Anxia (pronounced Anshi), who will interpret for us while we're in Beijing;

6

Mr. Li, a young man from the Foreign Office; and Mr. Lin, whom we remember from our other visits. He had worked out our schedule. We sat in our tiny, boiling-hot room (no air conditioning here) and heard the plans. One week in Beijing, then on the road, first to the northwest and then to Tibet—really a fairly rugged trip by train, plane, and car. I hope we survive. They said we might have to stay another day at the Airport Hotel because Beijing is so crowded, but around 4:00 they called and said a room was available. We got a taxi, and here we are. This hotel is air conditioned, though our room is a bit stuffy. But it's roomy, and the bathroom is nice. We are in the west wing, the old part, but not looking over the Forbidden City, which is just as well because the sun would be pouring relentlessly in the window during the hottest part of the day.

Tuesday, July 22, 1:45 P.M.

THIS MORNING right after breakfast we went to the Historical Revolutionary Museum in Tien An Men Square. This has been closed since the Cultural Revolution, we were told, and only opened last year. Harrison thought it had been open for short periods, but I don't see why they would say it had been closed if it weren't true. Liu Shao-chi was mentioned quite a lot, Lin Piao once, Mao Zedong a lot, and Zhou Enlai more than any of them. It was the usual collection of pictures and revolutionary stuff starting at 1840 and continuing up to 1949. H. is looking for pictures for a book he and

J. C. Suares are planning about China in revolution (they did a beautiful book, *Russia in Revolution*, a few years ago). He picked out quite a few, fifty-five in all, that he hopes to get prints of. Strange that there seem to be no posters. Most revolutionaries consider them the best way to attract attention and arouse the people, who so often are illiterate and uneducated.

We stayed there much too long for my taste. We got back here after noon, nearly four hours. We have had lunch—just soup for me—and will be taking off for the Zhou Enlai exhibit in fifteen minutes.

Across the square from the Revolutionary Museum is the enormous Great Hall of the People. It has a room for every province, including Taiwan, and is used for meetings and banquets. In 1972 we were guests of Zhou Enlai, along with other visiting American journalists, scientists, and professors. We met first in one of the huge rooms for tea and talk for nearly an hour; then we moved to another room and enjoyed an intimate dinner with that remarkable man. In 1977 we again attended banquets there, one given by Foreign Minister Huang Hua for Secretary of State Cyrus Vance, who reciprocated and gave one for his Chinese host a few nights later. And there we met former vice-chairman Li Hsien-nien for a long discussion, mostly about the Soviet Union and the threat it poses for China.

The Great Hall of the People has never been open to "the People" until recently. Now the general public is permitted to buy tickets for about 10 cents and enjoy a tour of the huge rooms. Today it was crowded with Chinese, and many more were in the museum. They were obviously curious about us, the way everyone used to be in 1972, and pushed and crowded to get a good look at such strange creatures. Most of them must have been from the country, for surely Beijing residents are used to foreigners by now.

Money: There is firm attention to money matters, and I have the feeling everyone is making sure we pay what we should. For instance, practically before we get to our destination in a taxi, the driver hands Harrison coupons that show how much we owe. And we noticed in the museum when we took a break in a reception room and were each given two bottles of lemon soda, only one of which we drank, our guide had to pay for all. And that comes out of our expenses.

The most irritating thing is that the Chinese have two kinds of money, *yuan* and *fen* for the Chinese, and RMB for tourists and foreigners. We can't use regular Chinese money. It is confusing to me, and I haven't got it all figured out yet, but I suppose I'll get used to it.

When we were discussing our trip to the west, and hopefully Tibet, Mr. Lin asked if we would sleep four in a compartment on the trains or if we preferred to "buy the four seats." Harrison doesn't want them to think we have unlimited money, which we haven't, so he said we would decide and let him know. But when we were alone, I said I couldn't handle two strangers along with us in such close quarters. We have too much stuff; there is no air conditioning; we'll be on the train two days and two nights; I am too old. If we go on trips like this, some concessions have to be made even if they are expensive. This will cost about $200 more!! But considering the overall expense of this trip, that is peanuts.

Wednesday, July 23, 9 A.M.

I MADE A calendar in the back of this notebook and have been scratching off the days. Already I feel we have been here forever, and it seems as if it must be more than Wednesday.

H. has gone off to the Military Museum, and I decided to stay here in our room, which now smells of insecticide. Just as well, since I have been killing cockroaches like mad. Not big ones—small and grayish, like those at the Savoy in London. It is so damp in the bathroom, especially after we have taken baths and I've hung up laundry. Cockroach heaven.

Yesterday, right after lunch, we went to the Zhou Enlai Museum, which is opposite the Great Hall of the People, as is the Historical Museum. There is much repetition of pictures, but it is a very interesting exhibit. In one early picture of Zhou he is dressed as a Chinese rich man, and he did come from a high-class family, the way so many revolutionaries do. Our guide said, "He did a lot of work with upper-class people."

The last pictures of him, when he was ill and after he died, with people weeping over him, were terribly moving and touching. What a loss to China, and to the world! He still seems to be the only member of the Chinese government, except for Madame Soong, with a cosmopolitan approach and understanding of some of the other people and countries on this planet. It was so awful that he was criticized and abused by the Gang's crowd and that he wasn't publicly applauded by the government and all the people when he was ill and dying. A terrible tragedy. And heartbreaking.

I came back before Harrison, hoping to fix my hair,

only to discover that the converter I bought in Hong Kong, especially for China, doesn't work here, so my little hair dryer is useless. Perhaps I can find a Chinese converter here.

We dined last night with Madame Soong. She is the widow of Dr. Sun Yat-sen, who was the father of the Chinese Revolution. She is also the oldest of the famous Soong sisters, daughters of Charlie Soong. As a boy Charlie Soong went to the United States to live with his shopkeeper uncle in Boston, to learn the business and eventually take it over. But he wanted to have an education rather than be a businessman, so he went first to Methodist Trinity College then to Vanderbilt University in Nashville, Tennessee.

He returned to China to preach the Gospel but soon gave that up to work for better conditions through industrialization. He imported machines and equipment, learned to install and run them, and worked in factories himself. And he became a friend of Sun Yat-sen.

He brought up his children as Christians and sent them to English-language schools. When they were ready to go to college, he sent them to the United States. One son went to Harvard, the two oldest daughters to Wesleyan in Macon, Georgia, and the youngest, Mai-ling, to Wellesley. The three girls married men who were working and fighting for nationalism in China, against the emperor and the feudal system of warlords. E-ling married Dr. Kung, who became finance minister for the Nationalists. Ching-ling married her father's friend, Sun Yat-sen, and several years later, Mai-ling married Chiang Kai-shek. In the beginning they worked together in the Kuomintang, the government formed to fight the emperor. Chiang broke with the Communists in 1927, slaughtering them by the thousands. Madame Sun went to Russia. The other two sisters stayed with their Nationalist husbands. At the time of the Revolution in 1949, Madame Chiang escaped to Taiwan, Madame Kung came to the United States, and today only Madame Sun Yat-sen, or Madame Soong, as she is also called, lives here in her native China, loved and revered by her countrymen, and a vice-chairman of the People's Republic of China.

Harrison has been corresponding with her for many years, and when we first came to China in 1972, she invited us to dinner. We saw her again in 1977 and have kept up the correspondence. We both regard her as a dear and special friend.

This was the third time we have had the honor of dining with this remarkable woman. On the two previous occasions our guide came with us and saw us safely through the big red gates guarded by soldiers inside and out. Last night we went alone in a taxi and had trouble finding the gate, since there were no soldiers to be seen and neither we nor our driver knew just where the great lady lives. There are other palaces behind other gates on this road, and we stopped at two before we found the right one. Inside each were two or three soldiers or guards, but it is certainly a more relaxed society than formerly, at least for some.

Our names were on a card at Madame Soong's gate, and we were admitted immediately. Two cars stood in the drive near the house, a Datsun and one we couldn't identify. It was not a Mercedes, as there had been on our other visits. The man who has always opened the door for us greeted us as before, and Mr. Yueh Tai Heng, the head of the China Travel Service, came in with us and signed his name, as we did, in the guestbook, (Later Madame Soong referred to him as "the host.") And once again we had the pleasure and delight of seeing that marvelous lady. She looked better than three years ago, and I noticed she ate more, something of everything, and always with a knife and fork, not chopsticks.

It was a family dinner, with Yolanda, Madame Soong's older ward, who is an actress and is to be married in August; Jeanette Sui, the younger ward, who came to our house in New York last winter, when she was studying at Columbia; Beth Wells, Jeanette's American friend, who is here with her now; Mr. Yueh Tai Heng, whose titles are "Deputy General Manager of the General Administration for Travel and Tourism of China," and "Deputy General Manager of China International Travel Service—Head Office." All that is on his card. Also the very nice woman, Mrs. Li, who has been Madame Soong's companion for years, and a Chinese woman who speaks English.

Dinner was served in Chinese American fashion. Three waiters were in attendance, and we had duck. Madame Soong said to H., "This is *not* Peking duck; they force-feed those ducks. This is Shanghai duck." At the last two dinners with her we had Peking duck offered with great ceremony. This meal consisted of clear soup with pieces of chicken in it; cold duck; shrimp, or prawns; cooked cucumber; fish; almond curd; and a birthday cake for Beth, which Jeanette had made. All delicious, and I tried not to eat too much.

Madame Soong is obviously happy with the changes in the country and with her young people around her. But she told Harrison that she has rheumatism in her knees and can't really walk at all. She has to be helped up and helped to sit down and gets about in a wheelchair. She would like to come to the United States but doesn't want to have to come in a chair. I don't blame her.

13

Harrison gave the presents we had brought, and I wish we had brought something for that nice Mrs. Li. They accepted the presents but did not open them. Madame Soong said of hers, "This must be Elizabeth Arden powder." I said, "No." She said, "Perfume?" I replied, "Yes."

We left early and were driven back in the car we still can't identify. It is air-conditioned, a real luxury.

This is a very different place from our previous visits. My *Travel Tips* of 1972 and 1977 are out of date. Downstairs in this hotel it is like a bazaar. Everything you can think of is for sale. All the Chinese items from the Friendship Store (the special stores for foreigners in every large city) are here—tablecloths and napkins, new scrolls, needlepoint and things to embroider, wool for knitting, jewelry, forks and knives, Thermos jugs, rugs, blankets, cashmere sweaters, embroidered blouses, beaded purses, fans, T-shirts printed with the Great Wall, bath towels, and even washcloths. There is a big assortment of Western liquor, a real change, including Johnny Walker scotch and Gordon's and Boodle's English gin. Many cosmetics, especially Max Factor.

Maybe all the big hotels are like this now. We haven't been in any other yet except the one at the airport. And we have never stayed here in the Beijing before. This is the main hotel for foreigners, and the turnover must be fantastic. We had heard that the service is terrible, the waiters rude and unobliging. But we are impressed by the service, the helpful attitude of everyone. The service in the dining room is quick and the waiters are polite as can be. Li told us, "Our leaders were displeased with the management of this hotel and told them they must do better." Sounds so simple and easy, but it seems to have worked here. The only things I could complain about are that the rugs are all stained, there are cockroaches, and the bathtub drain is all wound around with black hairs. I haven't quite had the stomach to pull them out—just added some of my own when I washed my hair!

We had lunch in a small dining room upstairs with Frank Ching, a bright, young, New York–born Chinese American who works for the *Wall Street Journal*. Harrison thinks a lot of him. Being Chinese, he is aware of lots of things foreigners and non-Chinese can't be. All the boring details of bureaucracy get him down, and it must be hard for him to keep a sense of humor. Harrison said, "This country and the way the Chinese operate drives most people crazy," and he replied, "Some were crazy before they came here."

It was interesting to hear what he had to say: that the Gang of Four will be tried in the fall; that it will not be a public trial; that Hua Guofeng will resign as premier but will retain one of his positions; that six vice-chairmen will resign; several "younger" ones will replace them —"younger," meaning in their sixties.

He said the new part of this hotel is bugged and that his family (and all Chinese) have to "register" if they visit him here. He asked the reason for this and was told it is in case of theft. "So you can question my family?" he said to the police, insinuating he realized they thought he and his family might be spies. They didn't like that very much. The worst is that he had a date with a Chinese woman one evening, and when she left this hotel she was arrested, taken to jail, and kept there for one week. Her father is a prominent official in one of the provinces, but no one knew that. When they finally found out, she was released, and perhaps it won't happen again. But this is horrifying, like the Soviet Union. Perhaps she is very rebellious, maybe even a dissident—but even so.

15

10 P.M., Same day

WHEN I went to take a bath before dinner, lo and behold, the hair was gone from the drain!! Did someone read this diary and clean it out? Too peculiar, but gratifying that I didn't have to do it myself.

Thursday, July 24, 10 P.M.

LAST EVENING a Chinese friend brought his wife to have dinner with us. We have known him since 1972, but this is the first time we have met any of his family. We had a nice time, and our friend answered some questions for me. (1) Yes, the Gang will be tried in the fall. Foreigners may not witness the trial, but it will be open to Chinese. That must mean special Chinese, not first-come-first-served. (2) Chinese people can travel around the country, go from city to city, or anywhere in China, without permission. But it is expensive, and they never can work anywhere except where they are told to. So generally they travel to see spouses and relatives who have been assigned to work away from home. (3) Families are still often separated because "work needs to be done in a certain place and the spouse's work is in a different commune, factory, town, or city. But the government is trying to remedy this." We heard the same thing three years ago. (4) I asked if students still have to serve in the countryside, factory, or the army before going to a university. He replied that the university facilities are limited and the competition is terrific, so only a few are accepted at any rate. But everyone can take the exams, and those with the highest grades go. (5) As to choice of what to

16

study and where, he said that students could list their choices, but he didn't say whether they went to a university of their choice or studied what they preferred. (6) He didn't answer about how many people are still sympathetic to the Gang of Four and its policies. We have been told that half the Communist Party is, besides many young people. (7) Off and on for the past few months people have been permitted to put up posters on "Democracy Wall", as they call it, stating their disagreements with the party and the government. There have been stormy gatherings, near riots, and at times people have been arrested. I asked about the young editor Wei Ching Sheng, who got a sentence of fifteen years for putting up posters and disagreeing with the party line of the moment. That seemed excessive punishment to me, but our friend said evidently he was guilty of selling state secrets. (8) In answer to who decides who will go abroad to study, the government picks some and pays for those. I believe each student gets $400 a month for everything. Anyone who gets a scholarship or has a sponsor can go and pay their own expenses.

I don't know how much of what anyone says I believe, but I do think the present government is trying to bring China into the rest of the world and make a better life for the people. One hell of a job! There is a lot of unemployment because there are so many unskilled people, and so far there isn't adequate means of training them.

This morning we went to the *Peoples' Daily*, the party newspaper, for an interview. It has moved from its old quarters to a big new compound with a large building for offices and equipment, houses for workers, and a nursery, kindergarten, and primary school for children. Really a wonderful system, in a way, making things easy for mothers.

Harrison says their equipment is as good and new as it can be. We were amazed to see it all work, turning out papers by the hundred, then going into a room where many women and girls were folding, stacking, and counting, all by hand. A mixture of old and new.

The deputy editor led the discussion, and I must say it differed from what we have heard before in similar talks. He spoke about investigating the oil rig disaster off the northeast coast of China in which many workers died. He called it a "mini Watergate." It took eight months of investigation, but they exposed the leaders who had lied about the reasons for the accident to save their own skins. They receive many letters from readers. He told how much money they make; the workers get bonuses and the paper keeps the rest and uses it—invests it in more equipment and magazines—to make more money. He said competition is necessary. "Without competition there is no progress." He said a few years ago he would have been called a "capitalist roader."

We had Ruth Coe and her two daughters for lunch. Ruth was married to Frank Coe, who came to China in the 1950s. He was one of the many Americans who were in trouble during the McCarthy days, and he lost his job with the Treasury Department. He died last spring and Ruth is still working for the Hsinhua News Agency. In the fall she is coming to the United States to see family and friends and to investigate other possibilities.

The two girls were born and grew up here. The oldest, Katie, is married to a German Japanese who is in Westport, Connecticut, working for Celanese Corporation and learning English. Katie works for the same company here mostly as interpreter and guide for visitors. Ling ling is seventeen and still at school.

After lunch we went to the Liu Shao-chi exhibit. Liu

Shao-chi was Mao's chosen successor but fell into disfavor and was ousted. The exhibit was put together last spring and opened on May 17, the day Liu Shao-chi was "resurrected." At the end it was explained that he was persecuted by the Gang of Four and kept in prison until he died. His wife was only recently released. Now he is recognized as one of China's heroes. The guide said he had written a report on "the shifting policy," which seemed apt. A friend told us that in one of the papers there was a description of the party line: a picture of a twisting line between two straight ones, representing the revisionist line on one side and the communist line on the other. The twisting line, going first toward one side then the other, is the government policy. How can people be expected to have blind faith, or any faith, in such a government?

In the late afternoon H. met and talked with Anna Louise Strong's great-nephew, Tracy Strong, and his wife. Both are professors in the United States and are working on a biography of his great-aunt. Anna Louise Strong was an American whose left-wing sympathies led her from the IWW in Seattle to Moscow and China. She was a friend of Borodin, Mao, and Zhou Enlai and spent her last years living and writing in Beijing. The Strongs have access to all her things here and in Seattle, but there is no way they can get anyone in the Soviet Union to talk to them about her because she came over to the Chinese side. So crazy.

We dined at the American Embassy with Carpenter Roy, the *chargé*, Mr. Thompson, also from the Embassy, and Mrs. Engelhart, whom we have met in New York, and her daughter. Carpenter Roy is very smart, and they were friendly and hospitable to us. The people in our Embassy all speak Chinese, except the ambassador, Mr.

Woodcock. He is away. Mr. Thompson is married to a Chinese American girl, but the wives were not at dinner. It was pleasant and relaxing; I had a real gin and tonic. Only in the room where we sat before dinner and also ate was there an air conditioner—very modest compared to some American embassies I've been in. The food was Chinese, and delicious, and it was nice to have regular red wine, not the sweet Chinese kind.

Conversation got around to the election at home, and Carter, and everyone seems to feel the same despair. There was a lot of talk about the Chinese and all the changes that seem imminent—that Hua will step aside and the older vice-chairmen will resign. Harrison feels that the great emphasis on Hua in the Military Museum may be significant in spite of all the talk.

Mr. Roy drove us home, and when we got upstairs, there was Mr. Mao, our interpreter and guide from 1977, waiting for us in the hall. He looked much healthier than he did when we were traveling together and was his cheerful self, accepting with typical Chinese stoicism his bad luck in missing out on two trips to the United States and Europe in the last year.

Saturday, July 26
Beijing

THIS MORNING we called on Mr. Wang, the head of the China Friendship Society, to discuss the possibility of a meeting in the United States of Chinese and American writers. Norman Cousins is trying to arrange it and H.

brought some messages from him. Mr. Wang is the diplomat who participated in all the talks in Warsaw between the Chinese and the United States, trying to solve their differences. We had a pleasant conversation and perhaps something will come of it.

The Friendship Society is housed in the main building of the old Italian Embassy. (Rewi Alley lives in his great apartment in this compound, the same apartment Anna Louise Strong lived in until her death.) The building is sad, as are the grounds. We had seen it before from the outside, shabby and neglected. Inside it is drab and grubby, though the windows, fireplaces, and moldings make one realize how pretty and chic it must have been when the Italians lived here. Neither Anshi, our translater, or Li knew that it was the former Italian Embassy. I thought that was peculiar, showing their lack of knowledge of history, or anything before the Revolution, and also their lack of curiosity. But H. reminded me that when he taught a seminar at a girls' college at home a few years ago, to his students, Munich meant only the Olympics. Their history began with John F. Kennedy.

We had lunch by ourselves—a Western meal that was the speciality of the day in the dining room, string beans and hamburger. And later I met with four women of the Womens' Federation of China. This organization was set up in 1949 after Liberation and is really an outgrowth of a similar group that existed before 1919. During the May Fourth Movement era it consisted mostly of students. (The May Fourth Movement began with a demonstration of several thousand students in Beijing on May 4, 1919, against the Versailles Peace Conference decision concerning Shantung. This was a complicated question involving past treaties and agreements with the United States, the European Allies, Germany, and Japan, resulting in Japanese control of what the Chinese considered their "Holy Land," since Shantung was the birthplace of Confucius.) It was mainly an organization of workers, sometimes referred to as Womens' Liberation, and during the Sino-Japanese war in the thirties it was called the Salvation Unit. In the early days only 7 percent of Chinese workers were women; today they make up one-third.

Of course, it is impossible for me to meet anyone I want and ask all the questions I would like to ask, but this turned out to be interesting because of the head lady, Mrs. Dong Bien. She is a strong-spirited woman with an amazing past, at least to me, an American, though not too unusual for China. She was the third daughter of a landlord, and when she was born and the terrible fact that she wasn't a boy was revealed, she was put out in a box in the water to drown. Someone found her and returned her to her family, who believed she was a devil and that her birth had prevented her mother from having a son. They treated her cruelly and didn't allow her to go to school; finally she ran away. She joined the army and from then on worked in various women's movements and groups. She took part in military drills and learned guerilla warfare. She didn't actually fight, but she worked against the Japanese in the thirties, and later against the army of Chiang Kai-shek. During these years with the army she became pregnant and had a baby, which she gave to a village family. She was unemotional and practical about this; it was a common occurrence. The young mothers cared so much about their country and what was happening to it, and they couldn't be both mothers and soldiers.

She didn't communicate with her family for many years. After 1949 their land was confiscated and divided up into three hundred households.

The other three women had important positions in various branches of different organizations, all under the aegis of the encompassing federation. One works with a family program that stresses and advises families to (1) study; (2) work well; (3) educate children; (4) be a united family, don't fight; (5) do a good job in sanitary work.

If I were a more experienced interviewer, I would have sensed right away that Mrs. Dong was the most interesting and concentrated on her.

After the interview we went to see Mao Zedong in his tomb. It is in the huge mausoleum in Tien An Men Square that was opened three years ago just as we were leaving Beijing. So we have never seen the inside. Many old houses were torn down to make room for it. Strangely, the entrance faces north and Chinese buildings and houses have always faced south, as they do in Sikkim. It was based on a superstition and the feeling it was bad luck to face any other way.

Seeing Mao was a pretty quick procedure. We stood outside with all the other people waiting to see him for about five minutes before the line started to move. Not as in Moscow, where Russians wait for hours to see what's left of Lenin in his tomb in Red Square, and foreigners are whisked through ahead of people who may have been waiting for half a day or more.

When we entered the door, the line separated, some to the left, some to the right, reminding me of marching in the gym at the Winsor School. (I wonder if children do that anymore. I used to love it—marching to music, round and round, in and out, making all sorts of formations.)

We met our fellow sightseers behind the main entrance room in a hallway from which we went into the tomb room, separating again, with a group on each side, to see the body. Two police, or guards, stood on each side of the entrance, two more on each side of the tomb, and four behind, or at the head of the tomb, facing the crowd as we came in, so they can see everyone all the time. I noticed how quickly the guards reacted when a man put on his glasses and leaned over the rope barrier to get a better look at the body. A constant watch was kept on him.

Mao is not a very impressive sight. He lies on a slab within a glass case, or dome, and is covered so that only his chest and head show. He doesn't have the smooth, un-wrinkled look of a dead man; he looks more as if he were made of papier-mâché painted to look like skin. We heard that the authorities couldn't decide whether to exhibit him this way or not, and took a long time making up their minds. Someone said *he, Mao,* took a long time to make up *their* minds, meaning that he was still telling people what to do even when he was dead. A Japanese embalmer was employed, but perhaps he was too late. He certainly didn't do a good job, maybe on purpose, maybe because he wasn't competent, or maybe it just wasn't possible.

I can't help but compare Mao's corpse with Lenin's. Compared with Lenin, Mao looks 100 percent unreal. Every time we see Lenin, he seems to have shrunk a bit, but he looks as if what we see was once alive, and Mao doesn't look like that to me. Such a bizarre custom—to preserve and exhibit a dead body! It seems unfair to the person, and so undignified, like a side show in a circus. And what will they do with the poor thing if it is decided that Mao was responsible for the Cultural Revolution and the Gang of Four? Will they remove him some night, the way the Russians did Stalin? Who will they put in his place? An American girl told us she was told by a Chinese that every night Mao is cranked down out of the glass dome to a sort of deep freeze compartment because his body isn't in very good shape and this will help preserve it and keep it from deteriorating further. This might also be for security reasons. It was pretty cold in the mausoleum but not freezing.

We had dinner with Arthur Golden, who dined with us in New York the night we had Jeanette Sui at our apartment. He is here for the summer, living at the university and studying Chinese. He is Ruth Holmberg's son and Iphegene Sulzberger's grandson. He took us to the Mongolian restaurant at the edge of the lake near Madame Soong's. Across the little bridge you go left to all those walls and gates shielding the palaces from public view, then right to a busy street of shops and people bustling about. The restaurant has existed as a restaurant in this same place for several hundred years. We sat on the upstairs balcony and watched people swimming and boating on the lake while we had a dinner that seemed more Chinese than Mongolian.

From there we went to the Peking Opera to see *Monkey*, or *Monkey King*. We were surprised when the taxi let us off in front of a big theater near the Chien Men Hotel, our first home in Beijing in 1972. At that time, and until recently, this theater was closed. Chiang Ching, who had made herself the cultural boss of China, didn't like the old operas, thought they were antirevolutionary and reactionary. They were not shown anywhere in China during the Cultural Revolution and her reign of power in spite of the fact that *Monkey* was one of Mao's favorite stories. "Never underestimate the power of a woman," as the *Ladies Home Journal* used to say.

Until tonight I had only seen bits and pieces of the Peking Opera, in Hong Kong and, more recently, in New York. It is just the most wonderful collection of fairy tale imagination; of travelers in the desert along the old Silk Road (where we will be heading tomorrow); bandits; robbers; good people; bad people; a beautiful girl in distress; her rescue; and the wild unpredictable Monkey, who is featured so much in Chinese fairy tales.

The costumes are gorgeous and elaborate, as are the sets. The actors talk and sing in a very stylized manner to the accompaniment of high-pitched music, much clashing of cymbals, and something that sounds like castanets, only louder. Every movement, every turn of a hand or an arm, each swish of a skirt or coat, has a special significance.

Another surprise was the audience. The theater was packed. It was boiling hot and many men were in their undershirts. Everyone had a fan, and in the intermission there was a mad dash for the popsicles being sold in the lobby. I would have thought that the average Chinese working person who has not seen anything like this opera for years, if ever, would find this lavish production baffling and meaningless, maybe even boring. It is so completely different from the revolutionary plays and ballets all full of party propaganda, which were the only entertainment for many years. But, without exception, they leaned forward in their seats, followed every word, knew just what was happening, cheered or booed in the appropriate places. Clearly they are familiar with the old fables even if they were out of style and forbidden for so long.

Sunday, July 27
3 P.M., Beijing

THIS MORNING, with some Chinese friends, we strolled around in the Forbidden City. If I were to go there every day, I am sure I would never get used to this fabulous place. Going through the big Gate of Heavenly Peace and seeing that first huge building, the Hall of Supreme Harmony, gives me the same sensation as going through that other gate and seeing the Taj Mahal all at once, in all its splendor right there in front of me. The revolutionary slogans that never seemed appropriate on the big red walls, have been painted over and the buildings are being repainted and kept up. Many Chinese were enjoying it as we were.

We have packed up all the junk we brought, once again wishing we'd brought nothing but the clothes on our backs. If we hadn't embarked on such a long trip, I wouldn't have brought so much. But it is hot here and cold at night in some places we're going. And while we need very few clothes for our time in China because I wash everything at night, we are hoping to go to Nepal and stay with our ambassador, and we want some changes. But it isn't really clothes; it's all the extras that make traveling more comfortable if we didn't have to lug them around: knitting, plastic coat hangers, a shortwave radio, and *books*. Harrison must have brought twenty-five or more. He has given away a great many, which lightens the duffle bag, but I bought some material and T-shirts, which take up most of the space emptied.

Monday, July 28
On the train to Lanzhou

HOT, STICKY. I have a cold, of all things I didn't expect.

This is a typical Chinese train, very long with lots of cars. There are three classes for travel, which aren't called classes anymore; soft sleeping, which we are in; hard sleeping, which is on wood bunks in the open, no compartments; and hard sitting. We have a four-berth compartment to ourselves. A table with a plastic cover is between the berths, and on it are a lamp with a silk shade, four teacups, and an ashtray. Underneath are the knobs for turning on the fan and loudspeaker. Curtains at the window are of blue velvet. Up over the door is a huge space for luggage, and even we can't fill it.

At one end of the car there is a washroom with two basins, and next to it a separate room with an Oriental toilet. These are oblong-shaped holes, generally made of porcelain, but right on the floor. A kind of spatter shield is at the top, or where you face, and two plates shaped like footprints, one on each side, are for your feet. You squat over these toilets. This one is surrounded by wood slats. At the other end of the car is a Western toilet, which is kept locked. We have to ask the car attendant when we need to go there, but I noticed a policeman take a key out of his pocket and unlock the door for himself.

At our first meal, Li, our guide, sat at a different table, but at dinner I suggested he sit with us, and he did. There are bars over the windows in the dining cars where the food is kept, and we were told to lock our stateroom when we left it. I saw a man attempt to board the train when we were walking on the platform at a station stop, and a railroad guard grabbed him off. It is more like home than like the honest People's Republic of China.

There is music on the loudspeaker most of the time, very little propaganda. It is an amazing mixture of American folk tunes, such as "Red River Valley," "Oh Susannah," "Clementine," "Old Lang Syne," a sort of polka, 1930 jazz tunes, and a combination of "Hello Aloha" and cowboy songs. While we were having dinner, some kind of drama was going on to an accompaniment of Gershwin's *American in Paris*. Harrison suggests that the person in charge of the music went to a mission school in the 1930s.

Whenever we stop at a station for ten minutes or so, the conductors, most of whom are women, get out with pails of soapy water and long-handled brushes and wash the outside of the cars. Inside they are constantly mopping the floors.

At night the car attendant doesn't make up the beds, but on each berth there is a pile containing a huge bath towel sheet, a blanket, pillows, and smaller towels to use in the washroom or put over the pillow case. I sleep on the large towel, which is really a summer blanket, rather than on the straw mat I've been sitting on all day. The attendant brings tea and hot water whenever we ask.

Every time I travel on a train such as this, I wonder why our transportation system is so bankrupt and limited; airplanes and cars make up most of it. Yet there is a real need for trains, for long and short trips. They can provide a comfortable, relaxing way to get from one place to another, but recent experiences at home haven't borne that out. Dirty, littered trains, always late or breaking down, are the rule rather than the exception. Too bad.

The railroad runs through countryside that Harrison

describes as "heavily and diversely agricultural." All different kinds of vegetables and lots of corn. Obviously there has been heavy rain recently, since much of the corn is battered down. I have seen very few machines on the fields, which are also of diverse size. As we go west, there are more and more goats.

Tuesday, July 29, 9:30 A.M.
Lanzhou

WE ARRIVED here early this morning and are settled in a nice room in a big hotel. We have had baths, changed our clothes, had breakfast, and, as usual, I have washed all our dirty clothes.

At the station there were pedicabs, chairs with awnings pulled by men on bicycles. It surprised me, it always does, to see people pulling other people, especially here. But Harrison says he is not surprised at all.

We drove a long way to this hotel, at least half an hour. This is a huge city in an enormous valley—very spread out. Mixed up with the modern buildings are primitive-looking cave dwellings. They don't have windows and doors like the caves at Yan'an, only a large opening or hole. On the side of the road away from the river are steep hills with old houses on the sides and tops, and very steep hard-packed foot roads.

Lanzhou, in the foothills of the Gaolan Mountains, is the capital of Gansu Province and just about in the middle of north China. The Yellow or Huang He River flows through it. From ancient days it has been an important link in communications with other parts of China as well as a stop on the old Silk Road.

As long ago as the second century B.C. caravans passed here, taking silk from Beijing and Xi'an over a tortuous desert and mountainous route through China to Samarkand, Baghdad, and eventually to Rome. Distances that can now be covered in a matter of days or weeks, then took several years. Overland trade flourished until sometime in the sixteenth century, when shipping supplanted it, being quicker and easier in spite of the risks at sea.

In modern times, under the present regime, Lanzhou has become the center for nuclear production. Originally this area was chosen because it is so far away from the United States, and we were the number-one enemy. Now things have changed; we are welcome whereas their former friend, the Soviet Union, is the current threat. But in 1960, when this latter change in relations took place, it was too late to move everything. So, here it all is: too close for comfort to the Soviet border (about 400 miles, [650 kilometers]).

There are several old springs and temples to see, but we will be touring the hydroelectric and chemical plants, I'm afraid. We leave at 10:30 for the former: 45 miles (70 kilometers) away. All day sitting in a car.

That night

THOUGH I HAD dreaded it, we had a nice drive to the hydroelectric plant. We went up, over and around mountains, very dry, like Nevada and New Mexico. Much terracing wherever possible. They grow a lot of potatoes, wheat, corn, many kinds of vegetables, and thirty dif-

31

ferent kinds of apples. This area is famous for melons, especially honeydew, seeds of which Henry Wallace sent from the United States in 1944, when he visited here and saw what perfect conditions exist for melons.

We had the usual talk with the manager, or director. He didn't seem the proper caliber for such a position. He told us the history of the project, not very interesting details. What is interesting is that China's nuclear defense system is in this area. We saw that the workings of the dam are inside a mountain; on the way to the damsite we both noticed a gate in the side of another mountain and imagined what was beyond it. Behind a wall we saw an array of antiaircraft guns, huge long things. On the way back H. saw soldiers engaged in a drill.

On our tour of the plant we noticed that all the signs on the doors were in English as well as Chinese: Dining Room, Meeting Room, Ladies Room, and so on. There were no party-line propaganda posters, only slogans about the Four Modernizations. This is the program set forth by Deng Xiaoping urging China to modernize her agriculture, industry, science and technology, and national defense. Of the 889 people who work here, 240 are women.

We went for a ride on the lake in a most comfortable yacht. Three electrical engineers from Beijing came along with us. One had been to MIT for three years and then worked at General Electric at Schenectady, New York.

The lake was made by damming the Yellow and the Haiho rivers. The reservoir is 35 miles (60 kilometers) long and 300 feet (90 meters) deep. The engineers told us that silt is a big problem and that so far there is no solution. On the shores strange red earth is topped by gray gravel, and rocky, nearly bare mountains come right down into the water. In only one place was it suitable to terrace and plant crops, and that wasn't very big. The water was clear and beautiful. People were fishing from three boats, and at one spot, several were swimming. It is amazing to see such an enormous body of water in such dry, dusty country.

After we got home to the hotel, we had dinner with the vice-president of the Foreign Affairs Department of Lanzhou. Quite a feast!

Only 10 percent of the population here is native. (Our local guide, Miss Chieu, is.) All the rest seem to come from Shanghai and other parts of the south and northeast. They were simply sent here when the Chinese started building this city into an industrial and nuclear center. How many of them must have hated it! At that point there was nothing. A whole factory would be moved here, all the equipment plus all the workers. Many families were separated, many still are. They can go home once a year, and some family members travel out here occasionally. Formerly there were about 100,000 people; now the population is 1 million. There seem to be enough young people coming along to fill most jobs. They say those qualified go to universities. At the chemical factory, for instance, they have living quarters, nurseries, kindergartens, primary and middle schools, plus a technical university. Scary, inhuman planning—people being bred, nurtured, educated, and trained as workers to stay in the place they were bred.

Wednesday, July 30, 3:45 *P.M.*
Lanzhou

POOR H. He has gone to an oil machinery plant in this
heat. It must be well over ninety degrees. This morning
at the petrochemical factory I decided that was enough
for me. I don't get anything out of looking at all that huge
machinery, and it is so noisy. It is interesting that so
many things can be made from oil: fertilizer, all kinds of
plastics, material, yarn for knitting, to name a few, but I
have seen all that in other factories—especially, last time,
in Taching. We walk around the huge machines, led by
either a man or woman in charge of that special area,
slowly and reverently, as if we were walking around a
cathedral. I would much rather have gone to the commune and seen how they grow vegetables. There is a
Lindblad tour here, and that's what they were doing.
They recognized Harrison and asked us for dinner, but
we had to decline regretfully, since we are going to a
song-and-dance opera.

There were many slogans on posters at the factory—"Learn from Taching," "Keep independent,
make initiative in our own effort" (a saying of Mao's),
and others in that sort of strained jargon. A lot about the
Four Modernizations—in Agriculture, Industry, Science
and Technology, and Defense. H. says this is a first-class
factory with first-class equipment. Also, they don't have
hundreds of workers when they don't need them, as so
many factories we have visited have had. We have been
told that unemployment is a problem in China, and as
they become more industrialized and mechanized, it's
bound to increase. On the big, flat fields of the communes machinery can be used, but only a human being,

34

with maybe an ox, can work the small terraced places we saw yesterday. So perhaps in some parts of the country people won't be replaced by machines.

Later

WHEN H. came back from the oil machinery plant, we met with the man who is in charge of city planning. Harrison wants to find out what is going on in the areas from here to the Soviet border—whether the Chinese are continuing the big industrial buildup that began when they were friends with the Russians. From what we heard, it seems to be leveling off. Our host from last night was present and was awfully rude. He acted just the way the landlords do (or did) in revolutionary operas and ballets. He slouched in his chair with his trousers rolled up to his knees. I know this is a common custom, but it wasn't exactly the place for it. He kept getting up and going out of the room; he was obviously bored with and felt superior to the nice planning man. I was bored, too, but kept knitting and knitting.

We had dinner by ourselves, stopped at the Lindblad people's table for a minute (they were having a big Good-bye-to-Lanzhou banquet), and then went to the song-and-dance opera, *Flower on the Silk Road*. It was lovely. Written in 1977, when fables and fairy tales became acceptable again, the story is taken from a painting in one of the Buddhist caves that we are going to see in Dunhuang. It tells of a painter's daughter who is abducted by a wicked circus manager and turned into a slave dancer. This terrible man is in cahoots with bandits who prey on travelers in the desert. There are holdups and fights, chases and escapes; it's too complicated to describe in detail. It is reminiscent of *Monkey*, and, like that opera, evokes the romance and thrills of the old Silk Road. Travelers and good people are beset by troubles, bandits, storms. Right triumphs in the end. The costumes are gorgeous, the dancing very accomplished, and the whole spectacle most appealing. The audience was like the one in Beijing, hanging on every word, obviously reveling in this beautiful entertainment. Tickets cost the equivalent of forty U.S. cents.

The theater is like all the theaters I have been to in China since 1972. There are no frills, just a big, plain, barnlike structure with cement floors and hard wooden seats. No air conditioning. Sometimes there are big armchairs down front for special guests, but I haven't seen any this trip. We go to the theater just like everyone else, and I must say I prefer it.

Thursday, July 31, 9 A.M.
On the train to Liuyuan

THIS IS QUITE different from the train we took coming to Lanzhou. This one starts in Shanghai and goes all the way across to Urümqi. It takes four or five days and nights, and it smells as if people had been cooped up in it for some time already. I am grateful we have a compartment to ourselves. Half of our car is "hard sleeping," which means the berths are just wood slats. There are stacks of three berths—not two, as in compartments—and the car is all open, no divisions of walls or doors. Passengers bring their own bedding. It is chock

36

full of adults, children, food. Most are going to visit spouses or other members of their families they haven't seen for a while. Several young mothers have new babies who will meet their fathers for the first time.

One young woman is dressed as I have never seen a Chinese woman in China dress. Her skirt is very short, way above her knees. It is made of white silk, which by now is rumpled and soiled. Her sleeveless orange-flowered top is also of silk. Her hair is short and curly. She looks terribly out of place and somehow sad, but she clearly feels she is very fashionable. Li said, "If we saw a woman dressed like that in Beijing, we would think she was a bad type." I wonder if there is much prostitution. H. says he thinks there's not much but probably a little, and certainly more than during the Cultural Revolution.

We have today and tonight on this train; we will go by car tomorrow morning to Dunhuang Grotto, where we will spend two nights. It is very primitive there, we have been told—no conveniences. Also, we have been told to be careful about food. It would be best to eat nothing. I am worried about us on this trip: It is not easy traveling. And I keep wondering if we will be able to get to Tibet—Harrison's dream. We are "old," though younger than many of the Chinese government officials; they say we have to have complete physical examinations, even though we both had them at home and have letters from our doctor; they worry every minute about the altitude in Tibet (it is 12,000 feet, [3,500 meters] in Lhasa). Our—meaning foreigners—blood pressure is higher than that of the Chinese, and they worry about that. Well, we shall see.

Friday, August 1, Evening
At Dunhuang Guest House

WE ARRIVED here this morning after a long drive from Liuyuan, about two and half hours in all, counting a stop of about ten minutes to cool off the car. We have a woman from Liuyuan accompanying us. This is still the custom—to have a local guide join us at each new place, and it makes a lot of sense. It also must relieve Li considerably; he doesn't have to try to answer all our questions alone.

We are just below the Gobi Desert; in fact, I believe we are actually in a part of it. Leaving Liuyuan, we first drove through sharp, gravely hills that soon flattened out to red and sandy desert. There is very little rainfall. July and August are the wet months, but there are no signs of rain except in a few scooped-out places next to the road. There seemed to be three separate communes in areas where they have been able to build some sort of reservoirs to catch the runoff from the mountains. It was amazing to see long lines of trees, wheat and cotton growing, sheep, goats, and a few cows, then more desert, then another green patch. Obviously there have been settlements in or near these places in the past. There are many remains of walls and dwellings as well as ancient watchtowers spaced one-and-a-half to three miles (two-and-a-half to five kilometers) apart. Fires used to be lit in these to warn of approaching armies or bandits. A fire in the first tower was seen by the next, so a fire was built in that for the one beyond it to see. And so on down the line. It took twenty-four hours for news to reach Xi'an, then known as Chang-an, which was the capital in those days.

That is a long way, about 400 miles (650 kilometers). Li said they used smoke signals, meaning small fires, in good weather; big fires of flames in misty weather. Drums were beaten in addition in really bad weather. If the wind blew the way we saw it was blowing out of the train windows, I don't think drums could be heard. The towers are made of clay and mud, and many have survived in remarkably good shape.

This guest house is like a motel and much nicer than I expected. There are several buildings of eight rooms, each room with door, window on the door side, and a window opposite between the beds, which are against each wall. Neither window seems to open, but there is a transom over the door, which does open. So far no bugs, but there is incense in the table drawer and signs that it is generally burned, undoubtedly left by Japanese visitors. They come here all the time, we are told. Five hundred are expected in the next week or so, twenty-five to a group.

The ground between the buildings is hard-packed mud. Inside, the floors are bricks and mud. It is like a cow barn, like the rooms we rested in in Silinhot (Inner Mongolia, three years ago). We have a Thermos of hot water, a carafe of warm water, and tea. And two huge enamel-painted basins, a kettle of water for washing, soap and two towels, and a spitoon.

We were told there was no toilet here, but there is a "bath house" with an entrance room that has two basins and running water. "Ladies' WC" on the left, men's on the right, each with two Western toilets and two shower stalls, all private, behind walls that come up to my chest in the toilets and a bit higher in the showers. So that's a comforting surprise, since I had expected something much more primitive.

We had lunch in the dining room, which is in a separate building: very good cooked vegetables and tea. There were two tables of Japanese, eating and eating and eating, and drinking beer, and a few English and German visitors. We sat at a big table by ourselves. Li eats in a different place, with the other Chinese guides and interpreters.

At 2:30 we set off for the caves of the thousand Buddhas. Around A.D. 366 a monk traveling through the desert came upon this spot and declared it holy. He decided to build caves in the side of the mountain and have them decorated with paintings and sculptures. Some are exquisite and well preserved, but too many were restored in the vulgar fashion of the Qing Dynasty, the last, which was terminated only in this century. The figures are coarse and ugly, the colors garish. And at different times over the years, travelers, armies, refugees, and bandits have camped in the caves, using them for shelter. Smoke from their fires damaged some walls and paintings. The Tibetans captured Dunhuang in 782 and held it till 848.

Over the whole outside is a layer of concrete, put on in the mid-1960s to keep the caves from collapsing. It is doing the job, but it is not very attractive. Perhaps something better will be thought of.

Sir Auriel Stern, a Hungarian by birth, was educated in England and became a British citizen. He worked for the British government in India. In the early part of this century he traced the route of the Great Wall, explored the Silk Road, and came to the caves. He discovered scrolls sealed behind a partition in a special room and took them all to England. His name is synonymous with "thief" here. As soon as he had made his discoveries, word spread, and German, French, American, all came and made off with whatever they could. I asked what the rectangular white space on one especially beautiful and well-preserved mural was, and our guide replied, "In 1924 a man named Warner from Boston put some special glue paper on that area and removed the painting. He also stole some of the early and best statues, which are now in the museum in Boston. The director of that museum was here awhile ago and said he was "sorry" but said nothing about returning them." Coming from Boston myself, I felt personally guilty.

Of course, the Chinese themselves, have "stolen" a lot, too. Many of the scrolls that Stein didn't find are supposed to be in private Chinese hands. And I can't blame foreigners for taking such treasures when the Chinese weren't making any effort to keep them for themselves. In fact, they didn't even know about their existence. Maybe it is terrible the way all people have made off, and still do make off, with other people's national treasures. But when I think of the damage done in all the war lord fighting, not to mention the vandalism and destruction through the years, especially during the Cultural Revolution, perhaps here it has saved some things. However, I think they should be returned now. I don't believe there will ever be a turning back to a feudal type of government or utter disrespect for the past and the history of China. The Chinese need tourist attractions, and this is a fantastic one. Also, they must be building up national pride in the accomplishments and art of the past. Our guide at the caves knew a lot about the paintings and the dynasties; she had gone to Beijing to study.

After supper back at the guest house, we walked to the museum and saw the few objects they have been able to gather together; some stone rubbings that are very attractive; relics from nearby tombs that were destroyed by peasants who "weren't educated to appreciate them." There were meticulous drawings of the tombs. This destruction by peasants must have occurred all over China. Artifacts interfered with plowing, and the peasants didn't realize the value of them.

The director explained the exhibits, and we had tea. I bought a rubbing on rice paper of a horse for sixteen dollars.

Saturday, August 2, evening
Dunhuang

IT GETS COOL at night here, and last night when we went to bed, we left our door open for a while. A dog was barking and barking. I loved the sound but wondered what it was barking at. Prowlers? Maybe the moon? The Japanese group left at 5:00 A.M., as we will tomorrow, and we are the only guests here for the moment. If that continues, I'll take a shower later. The two showers in the bath house have been occupied constantly by the Japanese ladies.

This morning the breakfast offered us consisted of two boiled eggs each, sweet coffee, warm milk, steamed bread, cucumber pickles, dried fish, and sweet cakes. We ate eggs—one for me, two for H.—and nibbled on the cake. Then we set out for Crescent Springs, not very far from here.

We drove right up to some beautifully windswept sandy mountains to where the car couldn't go any far-ther. We got out, left the driver sitting comfortably beside the car, and walked straight up a practically vertical sand dune, or hill. It was hard going; our feet sank deep in the sand, and I was glad it was early, not in the heat of the day. When we finally got to the top, we saw on the other side a valley with trees and shrubs and people harvesting wheat, right in the middle of the sand dune desert. With irrigation, deserts can be transformed into very fertile agricultural land, but it always surprises me to see anything green in the middle of so much sand.

We walked down the sandy hill and onto the flat fields. Several women were squatting among the newly cut stalks, picking up wheat kernels one by one that had fallen on the ground, and putting them in baskets.

We walked on over the flat, stubbly fields and struggled up another sand hill. On the other side, in front of us, lay a half-moon body of water, and inside the semicircle was a round place with trees and shrubs. The most beautiful surprise so far. It is impossible to describe. High sandy mountains rise up from this miraculously shaped oasis into a brilliant blue sky, all smooth and flat like a Georgia O'Keefe painting. Harrison says it is a floating island in a bowl of sand.

A local legend tells of a man who had "committed a crime and was exiled to this place to do agriculture." A magic horse had risen up from the springs, and the man tried in vain to catch him. Finally, he made a statue of a man and put it on the edge of the springs. Gradually the horse became accustomed to the statue and stood beside it when he came to drink. One day the man stood in place of the statue and the horse came right up to him, since he was not afraid. The man caught the horse and presented it to the emperor, who was so impressed by his ingeniousness he pardoned him. So the man left Crescent Springs and his exile.

Another story tells about a general and his army who

43

were camping on the side of the mountain near the springs. In the night a terrible wind blew up a storm and the entire army was buried in the sand. Gongs and drums were heard as the soldiers were smothered. They say now that if fifty people walk together on the mountain, the same sounds can be heard today.

Everywhere we go we are told an old legend or fable, and the operas are based on them. In 1972 if we mentioned a Chinese fairy tale or an old superstition, the reaction was, "There is no place for that sort of thing in our new Chinese culture."

A sad thing is that there used to be a temple here, right in the middle of the floating island, but it was destroyed by the Red Guards. A few years ago an irrigation project was begun here; the big stone foundations still stand. We are told it has been stopped because it would have been ugly and detracted from the beauty of the springs, not to mention spoiling the tourist-attraction quality. They say the stones will be removed. I hope so.

This is another change I notice from our previous visits. There is more attention to how things look. It is no longer considered bourgeois; it is, in reality, good business. It also seems to indicate that the Chinese are aware of the treasures they have and are starting to protect, as well as exploit, them.

Crescent Springs is an extraordinary place and could be very beautiful with a little care and attention. But I think they'll have to figure out an easier way to get there than climbing sand mountains. We walked back, around the hills, on a wagon track. But I suppose approaching that way wouldn't give one the real feeling of the desert and the wonder of seeing water and trees after so much sand.

I have never been in a desert before (we never got to the Gobi in Outer Mongolia), and I can't believe the sand, the wind, the dry air. How anyone survived those treks on the Silk Road, which went either through or very near here as early as 150 B.C., I can't imagine.

A short distance from Crescent Springs is the White Horse Pagoda, built by an Indian monk about B.C. 384–410. He was traveling on his white horse when it died. He built the pagoda on the very spot where it fell. It is a reddish, not very big Indian pagoda with something fancy on the top, like a wire with a few stones or beads hanging down. It is not in very good shape, and an ugly little shack has been put up right next to it, connected to it almost. The pagoda stands in the middle of a big wheat-threshing area. Huge stacks of wheat are piled up as it is brought in from the fields. A certain amount is spread on the hard-packed mud ground and a one-man tractor is used to pull a large stone between two rollers, in order to separate the grain from the straw. After that the grain is winnowed, then made into flour at a mill. The pagoda being in the middle of everyday life reminded me of pagodas I have seen in Burma. Except that nothing happens in this one: No one comes to honor anyone or anything, or to pray or to give thanks. It is just there, falling to pieces. H. believes it was damaged by the Red Guards. We were told that there is another pagoda in Liuyuan built by the same monk in memory of this same white horse.

From the White Horse Pagoda we went a short distance to the West Cloud Temple, a pretty compound behind a wall. Nobody seemed to know when it was first built, but it was redone in the Qing Dynasty and somehow not ruined. It escaped damage by the Red Guards, too, because people were living there; it was not being used as a temple. At present it is a grain storage depot, and we could only look from outside the wall.

After lunch we went again to the Buddhist caves and saw some really lovely ones in excellent condition. There are a few caves with the old original figures, which, even though they are damaged and there are missing parts here and there, are a relief after all those Qing Dynasty figures we saw yesterday. The best cave was number 272. It is small and has a round ceiling, None of the others are like that. The colors are heavenly and well preserved.

All the way back in the car I was thinking of the shower I would soon be enjoying. But when we got to the guest house, we found that a new group of Japanese tourists had arrived, and the ladies had completely taken

Buddhist caves in Xinjiang Province

over our side of the bath house. They were washing their clothes, washing themselves, washing their hair. It was hopeless for me; I went back to our room and washed in the tin basin.

Monday, August 4
Turpan

YESTERDAY, SUNDAY, we got up at 4:30 and left Dunhuang at 5:00. I hadn't had much sleep because after supper Saturday several of the Japanese tourists settled themselves right outside our door for an evening of beer accompanied by talking and singing. Harrison can sleep through anything—I guess it's a journalist's training —but I can't. Finally around midnight, I leaned out the door and in a plaintive voice said we had to get up early and would they mind going somewhere else. They were very polite and left immediately. Probably they hadn't realized we were there.

We drove back to Liuyuan in the minibus we had come in, over the same road across the desert, with Li and our local woman guide. She went to sleep and her head kept bobbing around like a real Chinese doll until I was afraid it would come off. The road is blacktop and just about straight. We met many trucks, some empty, some full of coal and other things I couldn't make out. There were trucks going our way, too. The Chinese have built three big roads to Tibet, and one of them goes off from this. Several caravans of camels were on the side of the road looking as they must have looked on the Silk Road two thousand years ago. The camels have two humps, like those I have seen in Mongolia. Occasionally we saw a desert dove and flocks of desert sparrows. How they survive is a miracle. There are practically no birds in China. In Beijing, for instance, I have never seen a bird except in Prince Sihanouk's garden, never any on the street trees or in the parks. There was a big campaign to get rid of them all early in the revolutionary days because they did so much damage to crops. DDT was used indiscriminately. Now, the Chinese realize their mistake.

Besides the trucks, there were wagons pulled by horses and mules and some donkeys. It is a busy road.

I have never seen a mirage before and didn't really see how such a thing could exist. But over and over again I saw large bodies of water far ahead of us and sometimes to the side. Big lakes, shining and shimmering in the heat. One looked like Buzzards Bay on Cape Cod, where I went in the summers as a child, and on that I saw sail boats. It would be easy to go nutty here.

We retrieved our big bags, which we had left at Liuyuan, had breakfast, and spent the day on another train, getting to Turpan at 10:30 at night, an hour late. This is the first time that's happened to us in China. Airplanes have been late, delayed, or canceled, but trains have always been precise. It was terribly hot all day, nearly 100 degrees. I slept some of the time, and when I woke up, Harrison asked me if I wanted some lukewarm tea. He says I answered, desperately, "I don't want anything—nothing." And a while later; "I can't handle this heat."

In spite of the heat the trip was interesting. We had a stop at Hami, one of the famous caravan stops of the past. From the train it looks like an old mud courtyard-house city that has grown enormous in the new Chinese fashion. We could see factories, irrigation ditches big enough for children to play and swim in; a stadium, and the three- and four-story buildings that make up every Chinese city I've seen. At the station passengers swarmed over the platform buying buns, pink popsicles, and the famous Hami melons. Before Hami we traveled through irrigated agricultural land, and also afterward for a while. But gradually it lessened and the desert took over except for a few spots of cultivation. We made two special stops to pick up sick or injured men. At the first, a coaling station in the middle of nowhere, a tall man in the regular blue Chinese uniform was helped to the train by two others holding his arms. A woman, maybe his wife, watched while he was helped aboard. Her expression was one of anguish, but she stood some distance away from him. She stayed motionless looking after the train until I couldn't see her anymore. How badly was he injured? Where are they taking him? Will she see him again? Another sick man was put on later, and after that a body, maybe dead, covered in gray plastic, was carried on. Life is hard out here.

The train radio had a larger repertoire than we heard on the Beijing train. "My Old Kentucky Home," "Ole Black Joe," "Drill Ye Tarriers Drill," Strauss waltzes, "Roll Out the Barrel," "La Cucaracha," "Jingle Bells," "The Impossible Dream," and "The Man of La Mancha" have been added.

At Turpan we were met by a friendly, large man, a Uygur, and a Uygur girl, who wore a light green gauzy short dress trimmed with silver thread and clearly

49

outlining her ample proportions. The minority nationalities are now permitted to wear their own kind of clothes, follow the faith of their choice, and have as many children as they want. No family planning for them.

The Han Chinese people make up 94 percent of the population of the People's Republic of China. The remaining 6 percent consists of fifty different minority groups of varying size. The largest, each claiming over 1 million, are the Mongolian, Hui, Tibetan, Uygur, Yi, Chuang, Puyi, Korean, and Manchu. Others have a thousand, some merely hundreds. For the most part, the minorities live in the border areas. The Chinese are making an effort to keep them happy; they can follow their own customs, have their own language, and go to their own grade schools. But after that they must attend Chinese schools and study in the Chinese language. Politically they are not independent.

Uygurs are like the Kazaks, and Mongols, and other peoples who live in this central part of Asia. They have broad foreheads, high cheekbones and generally, dark complexions. From what I have seen, they come in all sizes and shapes.

Turpan is in a depression that is below sea level and surrounded by mountains so the heat cannot escape. It is called the Oasis of Fire, it is so hot. The mountains are known as Flame Mountains because when the sun shines on them, the red sand and rock formations look like real flames of fire tearing up into the sky. We couldn't see any of this last night, but at the station a terrible wind was blowing and everything looked black and dusty. I was praying we would get to wherever we were to stay quickly, but this guest house is 25 miles (40 kilometers) from the station and it took two hours to get here. It seemed like the longest drive I have ever known. When we finally arrived, we were led to a terrace under a grape arbor, where a table was set and laden with watermelons. It really looked very pretty, but all I could think of was going to bed. Watermelons grew wonderfully here, and they are better than any I have ever tasted. So, we had a few slices, made some conversation, and finally were allowed to retire.

This place makes the Dunhuang guest house seem like the Ritz. Harrison dreamed about the Okura Hotel in Tokyo last night (one of our favorite hotels in the world), and it is surely only a dream. We have the same kind of cow-barn bedroom except there is a nice rug between the beds. It is less private than Dunhuang because rooms open off both sides of a central hall in a long one-story building. The bathroom for everyone is at one end—men's and women's sides separated by a partition about six feet high. Miraculously, there is running water. Or rather, was. When we returned from our trip this morning, the door was locked, it's all out of order. So we have to go a long way to the special house for such matters, men on one side, women on the other, both over the same ditch. You can't imagine the smell. A roll of pink toilet paper was on the table in the corridor of the guest house for people to help themselves. It soon vanished. A big French group is here. I wonder how they like it.

We have gone back to washing in tin basins in our room. Water comes from a tap outside the front door. It splashes into a cement-covered hollow and runs into a ditch that goes around the grape arbor. People empty their basins, brush their teeth, wash their clothes and even their hair here by the entrance. I, too, empty our dirty water out here; I don't wait for someone else to do it. We can get hot water from the room where they boil it and fill the Thermos jugs.

While guests sleep in the same building, and so does Li and other Chinese, we are segregated for meals. The food is the same for all guests, though I don't know about the Chinese. The French group eats in a dining room on one side of the walk between two buildings, and we eat in a small, airless, grubby room in the building opposite. We sit on low stools at a high table and even tall H. can scarcely see over his plate. We feel like little children at a grown-ups' table. So far I haven't liked the food and haven't eaten much. For breakfast this morning I had a few peanuts and some watery coffee with watery milk.

After that strange breakfast we drove to an ancient city that flourished from the first century to the fourteenth. It is all ruins except for a small square temple and a dome-shaped building, which are being renovated. It is just a big area of broken walls and remains of stupas (Buddhist monuments generally containing remains or relics). Early stupas were round and often of earth. Later ones are round but with a spire or steeple, more like a small pagoda. (These are made of clay or stone.) There is no color, only the brown, sandy desert color. Even through the dusty haze we could see that the mountains look as if they were on fire.

Then on to see some tombs in a big flat area where there are many round mounds of earth, obviously each a tomb. Only three are open. A little girl of about ten is the caretaker. She led us to the entrance, unlocked the door, and accompanied us inside. They are small and have practically nothing in them. There were four lovely, simple murals of birds and flowers in one and pictures of people in another. The colors are well preserved. A few bowls and utensils that the dead might need in the next life were all that was left. The third grave contained only five mummified skeletons lying in a heap on the floor.

Tomb entrance

They are in pretty bad shape. We were told that the best skeletons are in the museums of Beijing and Ürümqi, but also, we were told that there never had been bodies in the tombs we saw, which seems pretty ridiculous to say. I imagine the grave-robbing through the years has cleaned them out. Several tombs look as if they had been opened and then abandoned, since the sand has half filled in the excavation to the doorways.

From the tombs we drove quite a distance to another ancient cavesite high up on a beautiful river that runs through the valley between red, fiery sand mountains. Below the caves a house with a flat roof snuggles on the bank surrounded by vegetables and flowers growing in profusion. Children were playing on the roof. It seemed unreal to be in the middle of so much sand and dust on every side and look down on clear rushing water and so much vegetation. No wonder the traveling Buddhist monks considered these places holy and built and decorated these caves!

They must have once been beautiful with exquisite paintings, but there's not much left to see. After the Buddhist monks and painters, the Muslims came and, because it is against Muslim law to represent the human face and figure, they smeared mud on or scratched out every face and as many bodies as they could. Also, the Chinese say the British stole many murals from here—"cut them out."

Inside a large cave with nothing at all left on the walls or ceiling, we sat at a long table and had watermelon and tea. Then back to the guest house, lunch in our dreary dining room, and a rest until 5:00.

Feeling somewhat refreshed after a good nap, we visited a Uygur family in the grape commune. As is always the case when we are taken to visit people, this family lived in a substantial house and everything was spruced up. It was really very nice and the lady of the house was beautiful the way Mongol women are: black hair, high coloring, and gorgeous eyes. The Uygurs are Turkic people, as are the Kazaks, Uzbeks, Kirghis, and many others who are spread over Asia from East Siberia to the Dardanelles. Their languages are similar, and they are Muslims. Many of them are incorporated into the Soviet Union, and it is clear that the Russians would like to have the Uygurs, too. They broadcast especially to them: anti-Chinese, pro-Soviet propaganda. That's probably why the Chinese are trying to keep the Uygurs content and are letting them have what H. calls this "childlike, nonharmful, tiny nationalism," meaning they can have some of their customs, do their own dances, sing their own songs, and go to the mosque. We are told that mosques are being rebuilt here in preparation for a three-day pilgrimage later this month.

We walked through the entrance with the kitchen on one side, into a big, square courtyard. To the left was a banquette about eighteen inches high and as big as two double beds. Three great carpets were spread on it, and when we came, our hostess unrolled a flowered cotton-quilted long pad. We took off our shoes and sat on the pad on top of the carpets. When we had tea and grapes, another piece of printed cotton cloth was spread in front of us as a tablecloth. We had been told by someone in Beijing that we shouldn't eat grapes or dates, the two fruits this district is most famous for, but I find it absolutely impossible to refuse to eat what's offered at times like this. So I ate a few. They were big and green and seedless and tasted delicious, though in another week or two they are supposed to be better.

Over the courtyard was a trellis on which grapes grow

and so keep out the sun. It is an ideal kind of house for the climate, made of mud, rooms opening off the courtyard, an upstairs over half the house.

This family has six children. One boy works in the commune, the oldest girl in a small electric plant. The parents work in the commune in the field. The income for the family is 1,600 *yuan* a year, approximately $1,072. Father makes 1,000 *yuan*, mother 600. There was no mention of the son's or daughter's salaries or whether they contributed, though they both live at home. The father is fifty-five, mother about fifty. The youngest child looked eight or nine. To my question of who looks after the little ones when a mother works, the pat answer was "There is a nursery, kindergarten, then school." But it is quite clear that this mother looks after her children herself, takes them to the field with her. There are always children playing and squatting in the vegetable patches.

Medical care is provided by the commune and each family member pays 3 *yuan* (approximately $2) a year for all care. With no family planning for minority groups, there are children everywhere: in the bushes, in trees, in the water holes, millions of them. The tots go naked— little brown, dusty bodies. I have noticed a few swollen stomachs. But there is an abundance of vegetables, so perhaps they are just fat.

The women wear a kind of smock like a maternity dress that they must make themselves on a sewing machine, or someone makes it for them. (As in many Asian cities, men sit at sewing machines in the marketplaces making clothes.) It has a round collar, a few buttons down the front, and is full from the gathers front and back that are sewed onto the yoke. They are made of all kinds of material and designs. Some looked like silk and are midcalf length. Sometimes they are worn alone, sometimes over pants. But the Uygur women don't wear the Chinese pants and shirt. The girls who work at this guest house wear skirts and blouses, and the girl who waits on us at meals is quite fair, wraps her brown braids very prettily on top of her head, and wears a short brown skirt and pink blouse. The head girl wears a blue corded skirt that looks pleated but isn't.

After that visit we walked through vineyards and saw a remarkable stone at the base of one of the flame mountains. Water seeps out of the inside of the mountain, down the face of the rock, into a little stream that is constantly running. It is very pretty with moss covering the rock, and it's hard to believe there is water inside these fiery mountains.

From there we went to a mosque, built in the eighteenth century, where, we were told, they have services now. We asked if people had gone to the mosque after 1949 and the answer was, "After Liberation there was religious freedom," which we know isn't true.

Tuesday, August 5
8 A.M. Turpan

LAST NIGHT after dinner we watched a show of Uygur songs, dances, and music, colorful and tuneful and much more like what I've seen in the Soviet Union than anything Chinese. One song was about the Motherland, and H. whispered to me, "Which Motherland?"

We sat out under the grape arbor, where we had watermelon when we first arrived in the middle of the night. It is a very pretty square patio with a paved floor. I suggested they serve meals out there instead of separating all the guests and making us eat in hot, stuffy rooms, where the windows have been closed since our last meal.

When the singing and dancing were over, the group came in, sat down on the sidelines, and one of them said, "Now we would like to hear from our foreign friends." Ghastly, like some hostesses I know who ask guests embarrassing questions and make them talk about what "motivated" them into what they are today. So awful if you feel you aren't anything. The big French group giggled among themselves; then two ladies got up and sang a lovely song in harmony in very pretty voices. After that their whole group went to the stage and sang together.

Li said we were the only other foreigners, and I should represent my country. So I got up, had Li announce that I had heard many of my country's folk songs on the train radio, and would sing one. They made me stand by myself on the stage, and I sang "Clementine" and "Oh Susannah." It probably was a pretty peculiar performance, but everyone applauded and I was glad I had done it.

Now it is 9:00. We have had breakfast and are about to take off for another ancient city. Whirling through the "Oasis of Fire" with the temperature close to 100 degrees, suffocating in clouds of sand and dust, one more day I wonder if we will survive. I feel a little shaky, which is always a bad sign. Well, off we go.

11:20 A.M.

BACK AT the guest house much earlier than anticipated because Li is ill. We are supposed to take the train to Ürümqi at 5:00 today, but I don't see how he can make it.

We went to the ruins of Gaochang, a city built around 400 B.C. It flourished until the fourteenth century. The dates suggest it probably was sacked and destroyed by the Mongols. The ruins are in better shape than the others we have seen, and there are even some statues of Buddha, not complete, but clearly statues, in several niches in the central temple of the city. The Chinese have made a paved road through the middle to the temple—thank goodness—because it is a huge city and I did not feel like walking. It was built on an island in a river. The bluffs formed a natural wall on one side, and on the outskirts opposite is now, and must have been then, a lovely green space filled with vegetables growing. We looked down a deep well in front of the temple. There is no water in it now, and no water on the bluff side and no water in a large lake nearby. What usually happened in this part of the world was that the conquering tribes sacked the old cities and demolished the irrigation systems, which were sophisticated and extensive. Before too long the desert took over, and almost everything has been buried in sand. But obviously, there is still some water in the riverbed at times.

We stopped for the usual tea and watermelon, and unwisely Li ate two pieces. H. did too, but I refrained even from tea. Harrison suggested we cancel any other planned activity, since Li was clearly becoming more and more uncomfortable. On the way back we drove through the marketplace, full of people, donkeys, bicycles, those great wagon-taxis pulled by donkeys with a rug for the passengers to sit on and a canopy to keep off the sun; and fruit, vegetable, and bread stands—the bread those big, flat Arabic loaves. Many of the old men have long, pointed white beards and wear those little skullcaps.

Harrison says there is no essential difference in this present civilization and that of the ancient, ruined cities we have seen, in agriculture and irrigation. The standard of life has been improved by the Chinese introduction of modern sanitation, public health, and medicine; by train and truck connections with the rest of China; and probably somewhat by education. But the elements of daily life haven't changed much. Children up to three and four run about naked, splashing in the irrigation ditches and canals. People cluster in street bazaars to buy their food, jute or hemp, bits and pieces of iron. Trade is the same, donkey carts as they have always been.

5:15 P.M. — Miracle!!

WE ARE ON the train to Ürümqi, due to arrive at 7:15 this evening. A doctor gave Li some magic Chinese medicine, and he slept until we left for the train. He looks wan and ill and is asleep in the next stateroom. I feel okay but not my best. I am praying for a bathtub.

For some reason it took only one hour compared with two in the dark to go the same distance from the guest house to town. We stopped at the museum for a minute and saw some charming figures taken from the side rooms of the tombs we were in—with the pretty bird and flower murals. And some beautiful fragments of silk, several thousand years old. Why the Chinese don't use these heavenly designs on the materials they make now I can't imagine. And the subtle colors of the cave paintings.

The town of Turpan is one of the big coal and oil supply depots on this railroad, which has been built only since Liberation (1949). A lot of soldiers were on the platform and more Japanese tourists filled the waiting room.

This train is the Beijing Express. It is sleek and new compared with the Shanghai Express that we traveled on from Lanzhou to Liuyuan.

10:30 P.M. in Ürümqi

AT THE HOTEL everything is so heavenly I can't get over it. We were met by a lovely young man, Mr. Yang, who had the car right up on the platform next to the train. So there was no need to carry or drag our stuff more than a few feet. Li is still sick. Mr. Yang said that the deputy in charge of foreign affairs, Mr. Abdullah, was giving us a banquet and my heart sank. I didn't feel up to it and was sure Li wouldn't.

On the steps of the hotel as we fell out of the car, there stood two pretty girls in skirts and blouses, each with a bundle of wet cloths to refresh our hands and faces. Mr. Yang was very understanding when I said I didn't feel well enough to go to dinner with Mr. Abdullah, and he arranged for supper to be brought to Li and me in our rooms. I had soup and rice; Li had porridge, which here is watery rice.

We have a nice room, two comfortable beds that were turned down by the girl who brought my tray, and a super bathroom complete with fixtures that are spotless and that work. I have washed my hair, taken a wonderful bath, washed some clothes, and now H. is back from his dinner. Only he, Mr. Abdullah, and our new friend, Mr. Yang, were at the banquet. Harrison liked Mr. Abdullah a lot, says he is a pleasant, intelligent Uygur. He has met and entertained many Americans including Senator, now Ambassador, Mansfield, Senator Jackson, and editors of the *Wall Street Journal*. In the

Czarist days many Russians came here—Ürümqi is about 200 miles (320 kilometers) from the Soviet border—but Mr. Abdullah said the Russians are the smallest minority group. He also said that Uygurs can exchange mail across the border now, but H. seems to be dubious about that. The dinner was really a banquet: peanuts, dates, and bits of mutton *shashlik*, peppered and served with desert herbs. A watermelon carved on the outside and filled with fruit: bits of the watermelon, mandarin oranges, pineapple, and some kind of berry. Plus about twenty other dishes, all equally attractive and good.

Now to sleep. I can't get over being clean.

Wednesday, August 6, 10 P.M. Ürümqi

AFTER A good sleep we had a wonderful breakfast at 8:00. One omelette for us to share, not a huge one each that we can't eat, as we get in so many places in China; good bread sliced thin; fresh butter, not rancid the way most has been since Beijing; delicious pear jam; and funny thin coffee and thin milk, both very hot, that we drank out of wine glasses.

Li said he was feeling all right today so, even though we thought he should have stayed in, we left at 9:00 for White Poplar Falls, Li, Mr. Yang, H., and me in a car with a driver. The high Tianshan Mountains surrounding us are snowcapped and it is the most extraordinary thing to look up from the desert surface of red sand, black stones, and sparsely cultivated areas here and there to these great white peaks. The runoff is channeled in an irrigation system, and there is a lot of water even now in the summer. If it were not directed, it would just be absorbed in the earth and air. Driving through the valley it was like Montana: a rushing mountain stream tumbling through, the same yellow colors, and lots of what the Chinese said are pine trees, though they looked like spruce to me. Li said the trees had been planted since Liberation, but I can't believe that; they look too natural growing between the hills and mountains. But if so, what a task! It was a pretty drive, and when we arrived at the falls, the air was heavenly and it was nice to have a sweater.

We walked just a bit to the falls, which are like all mountain waterfalls: about 60 feet (20 meters) high and water splashing down over a rock wall into a stream. *But* there the beauty ends. This is a favorite picnic place for Chinese as well as foreigners, and I have never seen as many tin cans, egg shells, pieces of glass, paper, watermelon rinds, and so on. It is a disgusting sight in a naturally beautiful place. In one more year it will be like a dump. Obviously "the people" haven't been taught to take care of one of their most spectacular natural monuments, and I wonder if it will ever be attempted. I hope so. It is really sad. It makes me think of 1972, when everything was so neat and clean in China, no litter anywhere, and Harrison said, "Wait until they get tin cans and paper and all the junk we have, and then see how tidy they are." There were not even baskets or boxes to put rubbish in. I saw one girl sitting on a blanket on top of and surrounded by bones, broken glass, bottle tops—all the stuff I just mentioned. She was eating chicken, spitting out and throwing bones just beyond her blanket. I suggested to Li that the travel service should get the young people to clean up the mess and then have a stiff education program about how to take care of public parks.

Just below the falls is a settlement of Kazakhs (a minority group like the Uygurs), part of a commune. They live in yurts (round, collapsible tents similar to those of the Mongols) and take care of the sheep and other animals belonging to the commune. On the whole this outfit seemed more for show than for real. The yurts I looked in were spotless and had real beds, something I've never seen in a yurt before, but evidently traditional for Kazaks.

The French group that was at Turpan was there, and we watched a horse race together. Also the Kazakh horsemen demonstrated that horrible contest they have over the body of a sheep. There are two teams of ten men each. A dead sheep, minus insides and head, is thrown on the ground. All riders try to pick it up; one finally does and another tries to get it away from him. It requires as much skill, more really, of the horses as the men. The poor sheep is pulled and yanked, and when one man gets it away from the others, he gallops off, clutching it, with everyone in hot pursuit. They killed the poor sheep just before the game; H. saw them carry it down to the stream to clean it out. The French group were having a shish kebab lunch right behind the yurts, and the lamb they were going to eat was being chopped up by two men. The skin, with the head, lay on the ground near where the picnic was held.

I talked to one of the Frenchwomen, who told me they were not happy with the restrictions: having always to be with a guide; not having any freedom to do something different than what was planned. And they found the accommodations less than satisfactory.

We didn't share in that picnic—thank goodness!—but had lunch in a restaurant that was just a shed, and had some Chinese food for 10 *yuan*, about 6.70. A steep price. It should have cost about 2 *yuan*. I wonder if everyone is treated this way. Of course, most people go in groups where everything is all arranged beforehand. Certainly more sensible, and possibly cheaper in some ways.

But overall, it was a nice excursion and lovely to be in such cool air.

When we got back to the city, we visited the mosque we passed last night. The imam, or prayer leader, talked to us for a while, and I was fairly confused about a lot that he said. I gathered that there are twenty or more mosques in Ürümqi; they were all closed for one and a half years during the Cultural Revolution, from 1966 until sometime in 1967. He was abused and beaten by Red Guards, some imams were killed or died from mistreatment, whatever you choose to say. He never answered H. about how many people came to worship before the Cultural Revolution, how many now, and what is the difference? He said that many people can't come to the mosque because of their work, but in the homes the beliefs are strong and parents teach the children. He also said the people who came to the mosque are mostly old. He has been to Mecca, to Africa, Latin America, and other parts of Asia twice. He showed us inside the mosque, which is just a barnlike place painted the same light blue that is used in most hotels. I have no idea if this is typical of a poor one in a backward place or not. The imam says he is paid by the state, over 100 *yuan* a month ($67), a very good salary compared with what many Chinese earn. Some in the Foreign Office get only 60 *yuan* ($37.20). And I doubt if many other people here in Ürümqi, no matter what their position, make as much. It is obvious that the government pays him because they destroyed the mosques, or permitted them to be destroyed, and prohibited any religious practice. Now they have switched the policy around, but there is no congregation or anyone else to pay the imam.

After supper we went for a stroll with Li, who seems to be feeling better, down the street to the other guest house. It is clearly for famous guests; it is a big house behind iron gates. We walked inside, since they were open, and a soldier appeared immediately to ask what we were doing. The planting is attractive and there are many flower beds leading to the front door.

Just before dark we noticed boys and girls and a man armed with large flyswatters prowling through the high grass and pine trees outside our window whacking at some kind of bug and putting them into plastic bags. We wondered if they were grasshoppers. No one we asked seemed to know.

I have been worried that we have had no word from home and the family promised someone would wire us every two weeks. We are so far away, and I feel so out of touch. I hate it. Harrison had the best solution and put in a telephone call to one of the girls for 8:00 in the morning Connecticut time, thinking of course she would be home at that hour. My grandson Silas, aged ten, answered the phone; without batting an eye, he accepted a collect call from northwest China and said his mother had taken his sister to a horse show. He added that everyone was well and said he would tell his mother we had called. Just as if we were in the next town. (We found out when we got home that the call cost $12.)

So I feel better, but we will call again when we know Rosina will be home.

Thursday, August 7, 8:45 A.M.
Ürümqi

WE, OR RATHER I, "made a mistake," as the Chinese are always saying, and thought breakfast is at 8:00. So we were up and ready, but it's at 9:00. We went for a walk in the lovely cool air and I am sitting on my bed now looking at thick, black smoke coming out of two stacks of a factory not too far away. So far we have not smelled it, but it looks as if it were wending its way toward us now.

Three weeks from today we leave China—that is, if we go to Tibet. I am as much as I ever will be in the swing of traveling in this country, and barring sickness or accident, the next weeks should go more or less smoothly.

I forgot to write last night that all the theaters we have seen in northwest China are showing Charlie Chaplin movies. *The Great Dictator* is here in Ürümqi, *Modern Times* was at Turpan. Another popular one is *Nightmare*, a film about our South and all the inequalities there. Tickets to movies cost the equivalent of 20 cents.

Evening

WE SET OFF at 10:00 this morning for Tianchi, or Lake of Heaven, two hours from Ürümqi. When we turned off the main road onto a gravel or stone road, we saw a new kind of tree growing along the lovely, rushing stream. "A kind of Chinese elm," Li said. Soon the evergreens began, and in this area they grow very tall and thick. The placement of trees on the mountains is exactly the same as at White Poplar Falls, where, we were told, every tree

67

had been planted since Liberation. Here, they say the trees grow naturally, which must be the case at the falls, too.

It was a steep, winding drive reminding me of Sikkim, except that the road is better, and finally we got to the top. We thought there wouldn't be many people because it's so high and such a difficult drive, but there were hundreds, maybe thousands, of tourists, mostly Chinese. The lake is "heavenly," as it is called, and the setting is spectacular, but it is a worse mess than the falls yesterday. People picnicking, sitting in the midst of cans and broken bottles, throwing melon rinds and anything else they didn't want into the lake, music blaring from radios. Not only the Hong Kong Chinese have these, many native Chinese do. People selling grapes, tea, pop, cakes. Private enterprise photographers soliciting willing customers and cows ambling idly here and there. The rocks are very steep coming up from the lake but a place for buses has been cleared and flattened out. We had a good lunch in a restaurant—just a room off the kitchen. It would have been nice to eat outdoors on a porch, looking at the lake.

Everything except the water was the same color, grayish-black, and the many people blended into the rocks with the exception of a few women's colored dresses or the green of the People's Liberation Army men. (So far on this trip I have seen no Army women, only young men. On previous trips they were as numerous as the men.) The water was a beautiful deep blue-green.

After lunch we started back, and when we got down to the more or less flat rocky road beside the stream, we were going much too fast. Either we hit a rock or one flew up under the car, and we heard a resounding crack. Oil was all over the road, and the crankcase lay broken and empty several yards back.

So we could go no farther. We waited there until two cars came along that had room for us. Our driver stayed with his car and I suppose someone will tow him to a garage in time.

We got our ride with a Japanese couple, a young student and his teacher who looked more like a romantic couple to me. They, Li, and I sat, or rather squashed, in back, and Harrison sat in ease and comfort in front with the driver. It is against the law in China to have three in front. Mr. Yang went with another car.

At Ürümqi we stopped at the shop where national minority products and specialties are sold. Some of the material here has better and more sophisticated designs and colors than what I bought in Beijing. If it didn't cost so much to ship things home, we would have bought a Mongol or Chinese cooking pot, the small kind that sits on the table. A charcoal fire is in the bottom, broth in the circular part that goes around the middle. Pieces of vegetables and meat and noodles are cooked in the broth and after everything is eaten, you drink the broth, which is delicious by then. We ate that way at lunch with Ernest Satow in Kyoto several years ago, and I still remember how good it was. Something like fondue cooking, but better.

Friday, August 8
Ürümqi

THIS MORNING we went to the museum, which has some marvelous figures from tombs, artifacts, and pieces of silk and other materials, but no skeletons, as we had been told at Turpan. Then to a rug factory. The women sit on low stools or benches in front of looms, the way they did in Sikkim. Some of the rugs are pretty, but I have never been keen on "Oriental" rugs. I love the ones we have at home, but they have deep, rich colors and are more beautiful and classier than any I saw here. H. says it is really a cottage industry. Many people make them in their homes. There is an enormous amount of wool piled up in the yard: huge stacks covered with canvas. There must be enough for hundreds of workers to make thousands of rugs. A new building is under construction, so perhaps more will be done at the plant in the future.

On the way back here we stopped at the department store. It is well stocked with everything imaginable. Some of the material is terribly pretty, and the kitchen utensils are wonderful. I wanted to buy several enormous tea kettles for the equivalent of $4 each. At home ours are never big enough, and we are always burning them out. I bought black silk socks for Curtis (my son), and some cold cream in a pretty jar.

As everywhere in China, there is lots of traffic, from trucks to camel carts to donkey carts to wagons pulled by people. I said to H., "Where is everyone going all the time?" And he replied, "From here to there and back." Hundreds of trucks were on the road yesterday—all empty no matter which way they were going, except one or two that were carrying huge chunks of coal.

Ürümqi is the capital of Sinkiang, or Xinjiang, Province, the westernmost part of China. It comprises one-sixth of the total area of China, over 660,000 square miles (1.7 million square kilometers). In the past it was a center for trade and culture, a melting pot of tribes, of settlers and nomads, of religions and philosophies. It was China's door to Persia, Greece, and India.

Up until 1949 Xinjiang had a feudal society with all the

evils accompanying that kind of system: slaves, tenant farmers, peasants who had nothing, landlords, warlords, bandits, beggars.

Russia was interested in this area as early as the nineteenth century, and the Soviet Union today would like to take it over. It is rich in minerals, and with irrigation it has a flourishing agriculture.

Ürümqi is a Uygur city being transformed into a Chinese industrial center. Factories ring the city, roads are paved, there is enormous growth and new buildings, the airport is international. The military is everywhere, reminding us that the Chinese believe the Russians will attack them at any moment.

This afternoon H. went to a farm machinery factory, but I skipped it. I still have a sore nose and bad cough. It isn't really a cold; it's from this terrible dust and sand. I don't see how anyone gets used to it. Yesterday we had to stop twice because the road was being tarred. A machine went down the middle, spewing boiling hot tar accompanied by huge clouds of smoke. Immediately men and women who were stationed about ten feet (three meters) apart on either side of the road, started shoveling gravel onto the tar. The dust was unimaginable and none of the workers wore a mask. I can't even think of what their lungs must be like. I keep a handkerchief over my nose as much as I can. I *must* get over this irritation or I won't be allowed to go to Tibet. The Chinese don't seem too keen about our going under any circumstances, and if I'm sick, it will give them a good excuse to say no.

Tomorrow morning we go to Ili, about 40 miles (65 kilometers) from the Soviet border, for three nights; back here for one night, to Xi'an for one night and time to see the clay figures, then to Chengdu, last stop before Tibet, if it works out that way.

Saturday, August 9
Ili, also called Iling

WE FLEW HERE this morning—a one-and-a-half-hour flight in a small plane. We were the only passengers not Chinese or Uygur. We sat in the front seats with the metal partition to the cockpit in front of us. There were no seat belts. I asked about that and was told, "No seat belts in the first row." We would bang into the wall or hit the ceiling if there was a big bump. It was smooth, comfortable flying, but many people were sick. It must be nerves or fright; it certainly wasn't from bumps and being tossed around. We flew up a wide, irrigated fertile valley with snow-capped mountains on the south all the way. Very pretty. The airport here is tiny and in the middle of a clump of trees.

Ili, being so close to the Soviet border, is closed to tourists. It is a nice, provincial, green town, with fewer trucks than we have been seeing and many carts and wagons. Russia and China have been in and out of these border territories for hundreds of years, vying for control, yet it seems to me they really should belong to the people who have always lived here, neither Chinese or Russian, but Uygurs, Kazaks, Kirghiz, and so on. There have been numerous treaties between the two big powers, but the Chinese say the Soviets are constantly violating agreements, trying to sow discord among the people and instigating incidents. They say the Russian border guards go into Chinese territory and have even shot herdsmen who were peacefully caring for their animals. Propaganda is broadcast from cities inside the Soviet Union, Tashkent and Alma Ata, saying there is no food for the

Uygur people, that they are not allowed to go to the universities, that religious activity is banned.

Our room in the guest house here is much better than I expected. The beds are long and comfortable and big enough to sleep together. We have a sofa with a table in front of it and a big bowl of the most delicious-looking peaches. The bathroom is beyond description, but there are tin basins. Only cold water runs from the taps. There seem to be lots of Chinese guests staying here, and I am glad our room is at the end of the hall so that people aren't constantly walking by our door.

After we were settled, we attended the usual "briefing" to find out the program for the next two days. It became so monotonous to me I left and came back here and went to sleep. H. is all steamed up about being so near the Russian border, and I wish I could share his enthusiasm. But I don't feel well enough to have any enthusiasm for anything.

After lunch Harrison went to a cotton textile factory and a knitting goods factory. I decided to stay in. He says the countryside and town are "stuffed with militia." And he saw lots of little children with Russian faces—lots of Russians, too. One of the local Foreign Office representatives speaks Russian.

Sunday, August 10
Ili

H. WENT OFF for the whole day at 9:00, and I stayed in and tried to get over this cough. Mr. Yang, our guide from Ürümqi who accompanied us here, told me many foreign visitors get this bronchial trouble, but that doesn't make it any better. I can't remember coughing like this since just before my first child was born. I coughed so hard I coughed the ligaments away from my ribs—very painful. But then I was only twenty-one, and now I am sixty-six. I don't dare take the pills we have because they appear to be closely related to penicillin, and I don't want to get an allergic reaction out here, or anywhere. So I steamed myself several times with the hot water in the Thermos jugs, took aspirin, and drank buckets of tea. I look green to myself, and if I were at home, I'd sit out in the sun and get some color. But people don't sit out in this country, they squat or stand around. Only in the heat of summer nights in cities do the Chinese sit out on the sidewalks on tiny stools. There are no lounge chairs, or even plain straight chairs or benches in what would seem to me obvious places to sit and take the air.

It is hard for H. to have me like this, but it is hard for me, too. I now know I should not have come on this trip. I felt in my bones it wasn't for me, but I didn't think H. would do this alone. But maybe he would have. Then I would have worried about him instead of his worrying about me.

Harrison didn't get back until after 7:00. He had a wonderful day and looked sunburned and weary in a healthy way. He said I would have loved every minute. I don't know about that. I am happy staying here in this room and have become quite fond of it.

H., Li, Mr. Yang, and two local men—the representative of the Foreign Office and the Kazakh-Chinese interpreter who interprets for Li, who interprets for us—set forth in two cars. Both the latter speak Russian, which makes it easier for H., since he speaks it also.

First they drove to the old capital of Ili, about a mile from town. This site was abandoned in the nineteenth century because it kept being undermined by the river, so the town was relocated to where it is now. There they picked up two more men, the chief of police (H. thinks) and a Chinese army commander. These gentlemen, in their jeep, escorted the two cars, which means driving ahead and blowing the horn continuously to scatter the crowds, chickens, donkeys, and anything else on the road. When H. get out to take a picture, he said he attracted more attention than he ever has anywhere in China. He felt there must be a million people following him.

He sampled a few kernels of field corn, the kind that is grown only for animals, and thought they were very sweet. He told the Chinese that we eat a small, tender variety, and they picked several ears and brought them back to the cook here. No corn appeared at supper, so we don't know what's in store, if anything.

The best part of the day they spent at Saryun Lake, two-and-a-half hours north of Ili. The water is slightly saline, so no fish live in it and neither animals nor humans can drink it. H. says it is beautiful, surrounded by mountains, about 10 miles (15 kilometers) long and 5 wide and bright blue. There are no tourists or picnickers, so no trash.

They visited a Kazakh herdsman in his yurt, which H.

says was not set up for them the way the yurts were at White Poplar Falls. It was a regular everyday yurt, clean but not fancy, with a sewing machine, radio, good rugs, and piles of embroidered towels and cloths. The herdsman has a wife and eight children, and he minds 160 horses. He makes 167 *yuan* a month, a colossal amount for anyone in China. The Chinese accompanying us were amazed and impressed.

On arrival at the lake they were offered doughnuts that had been fried in sheeps' grease and were wrapped up in a towel; very thin crusty white bread cut in pie-shaped pieces, and *koumiss*. Made of fermented mare's or camel's milk, *koumiss* is slightly alcoholic and has been a staple in the Siberian and Caucasian people's diet for centuries. It is always offered to visitors, and it is considered rude to refuse it.

Lunch was in the herdsman's yurt and consisted of a four-month-old lamb, boiled with the head still on. The Kazakh custom is for the guest to carve the head and offer pieces of meat to everyone on the knife. I have a picture of Harrison doing this in Outer Mongolia. Added to that honor, at that time, the host plucked out the eye with his knife and gave it to H. The *pièce de résistance* for the visitor. He was spared both these customs today and said the herdsman cut up the lamb well and quickly, finally breaking bigger pieces apart with his hands. It was tender and delicious and H. liked it, but I think I would not have enjoyed looking at the little head, let alone eating it. It's the same idea as a suckling pig, which I've had on occasion and have had similar feelings.

On the road H. said there was lots of military, and a man told him all the young people are in the army. Here and there he saw a Ukrainian, gingerbread-shuttered house painted blue, but he saw no Ukrainians, only suspiciously blond Kazakhs. All along the road wheat had been put out to be run over—the simplest method of threshing. After trucks or wagons go over the stalks, the grain is swept up to be winnowed. Straw is gathered into bundles.

The markets in the villages were crammed with people buying apples, tomatoes, onions, melons, and personal stuff from little individual stands. Free enterprise. Everywhere it was crowded and gay with a holiday spirit.

Monday, August 11
Ili

I HAVE STARTED taking the antibiotic pills, ampicillin, because I don't think I am going to get over whatever I have without drastic measures. I have had four pills already and am crossing my fingers and praying that I won't have any reaction except restored health.

This morning Harrison went to a leather boot factory, where they make 85,000 pairs of shoes and boots a year, mainly for national minorities. The factory was started as a cooperative in 1951 and is owned by the workers, made up of six nationalities: Uygur, Han, Hui, Manchu, Sibo, and Uzbek. Planned profit is retained by the factory, and the salaries are relatively high: 190 *yuan* a month for a woman cutter, 106 for director, 96 for the deputy. They have their own militia and are not connected to the People's Liberation Army, though the latter advises them on drills and tactics. They are under the jurisdiction of the Party, meaning the government.

I stayed home and wrote several letters I have owed for months and have been carrying around with me hoping for just such a day. For lunch yesterday and today the cook has made me some delicious soup. He and the woman who waits on table are so kind and so sorry I don't feel well it's very touching. In the large airy dining room H. and I sit at a round table big enough for eight people. A few feet away, and with a high folding screen between us, our interpreters and guides sit at a similar table and eat their meals at the same time. Since this separation is the rule in China, I am used to it, but it always makes me feel peculiar and very much the foreigner and outsider.

In the afternoon I went along to the May First Commune, where they grow glorious apples, melons, and grapes in addition to the usual wheat, corn, and other grains. Most of the people in this area seem to be Kazakh, but in this commune there are many Hui people. While there are differences in the physical appearance of the various people who live here, they are not so clear-cut that I can tell who is what. They don't look Chinese and they don't look Russian; that's about as definite as I can be.

We visited two houses that had been all scrubbed up for us, and they were nice and roomy. Everyone has grapes growing on an arbor over the courtyard, and most seem to have a plot out behind for their own vegetable garden. Also, they have animals of their own. Since there is no family planning, the average family has four or five children, so they say. But there are so many around I think they must have more.

Ili is a sister city of Alma Ata, across the border in the

Soviet Union. There used to be lots of Russian settlers here, descendents of the German peasants whom Catherine the Great in the late eighteenth century enticed to Russia in hopes of upgrading the slovenly, unproductive farming practices of the Russian peasants. They settled for the most part along the Volga and in the Ukraine and were known as Volga Deutsch. At the time of the Russian Revolution in 1917, and for many years thereafter, they moved eastward and crossed the border into Xinjiang to escape the Bolshevists. They never liked the Russians, who hated them. Though they are referred to as Russians here, they are in fact German.

After Liberation the Chinese urged the Russians to leave, and most went to Germany. Not many chose to go to the Soviet Union. H. believes there must be a number who stayed, and he has been suggesting to our hosts that he would like to talk to one or two. Finally they dug up one rather disagreeable Russian man, and we went to visit him in his house.

It was similar to the other houses we've seen, quite substantial, made of clay, clean and neat, and it seemed to have many rooms. He needs them; he has thirteen children, most of whom we met. There was no mention of his wife until we asked. She also is Russian, and they said she was up in the mountains with some of the children picking cherries and fruit to make jam. That certainly sounds Russian.

He, the father, was one of the few who, in 1949, decided to stay in China. He was obviously terrified to say anything, only answered questions in the briefest way, and he refused to let us take any pictures. The family speaks Russian, the father Uygur, but none of them speaks Chinese!! The children go to a Uygur school. It will be tough for them when they have to attend the

Chinese school. The girls, especially one of them, were so pretty and nice, terribly interested in my knitting and pulled back the curtains so I could see better. I can't help but wonder what the future holds for them. What can they do? Whom can they marry? Are there enough eligible young people like them here? There is practically no marriage between the Chinese and the minorities or between minorities.

For our last dinner here we had shish kebab, which was delicious; some green leaves that the cook grew himself, very much like spinach; and good red wine.

The whole point in our coming out here was for Harrison to be able to examine the border conditions closely, and in Beijing he was told that when he got here, he would get the details. He says that the people here talk broadly about problems but don't elaborate or explain, and it's been hard to get much that is factual.

Tuesday, August 12, morning
Still at Ili

ANOTHER DAY OF washing in a basin. I am so used to it now I get just as clean as with a bath, but totally without that nice relaxing feeling of lying in a clean tub. Here we have a bathroom complete with tub, toilet, and basin, but everything is broken and so filthy we use the tin basins. We are supposed to fly back to Ürümqi at 11:00, and I hope we do. We seem to go farther and farther away from Tibet, which, after all, is the real object of this trip.

8:30 P.M. back at Ürümqi
in the hotel that
seems like the Ritz

WE FLEW HERE in a cargo plane, a new experience for me. There were no real seats, just a long bench on each side, no seat belts, very little air or pressurization. The other passengers were all Xinjiang people, and many of them were sick as we landed. I am sure it is nerves more than anything else. It wasn't as easy to look out the windows as in a regular plane so I missed a lot of the gorgeous scenery of snowcapped mountains and the fertile valley.

We arrived here in time for lunch. After that I washed my hair and nightgown and wrapper that I slept in at Ili. I didn't go with Harrison to the university; I am still taking things as easily as I can, trying not to get tired, and hoping to throw off this cough.

H. talked with some professors. It is vacation until September 1, so no students were there, unfortunately. The professors told him that the university had been closed for six years in the Cultural Revolution and that two people had been killed in violent fighting. When it reopened, they were made to take students who turned in a blank piece of paper as entrance exams. According to Chairman Mao, this indicated the ideal student, one of the people. There were articles in the paper extolling the idea and universities had to accept students who then had to be educated in the fundamentals. This university has just finished with the last class like that, much to their relief. From now on applicants will take exams and those with the best grades will be taken. No foreign students are here, but they are sending one to West Germany. An Englishman and his wife gave some lectures last year.

81

H. asked if there were professors here who had sided with the Gang of Four, and if so, what were they doing now. There were some, and teachers who were against the Gang were humiliated and persecuted. Now they are all here together. I wonder how they get along.

The bills at Ili were beyond anything the Mongolians, who are masters at gouging visitors, ever did. Meals were far more expensive than at the Peking Hotel, almost $70. According to what we know things cost in this country, $20 would have been more appropriate. H. got furious and told poor Li how bad it is to treat us like that. No one likes to be taken in this way, and that's what they are doing at every turn. All the correspondents in Beijing complain of the cost of everything. The Chinese are too smart to do this Soviet kind of thing, and yet they're doing it. They have a different kind of money for foreigners and we have to use it; we can't use regular Chinese money. That's what I mind, being treated so differently from the way the Chinese are treated. We don't have special money for tourists or foreigners.

Wednesday, August 13
Xi'an

THIS MORNING at Ürümqi we got up at 5:00, had breakfast at 5:30, and flew here around 7:00. I was sorry to leave that pleasant place, an oasis of comfort in our traveling, about most of which I would not use the word *comfort*. We had a stopover at Lanzhou for over an hour, so we had lunch at the airport.

Li came with us to the restaurant, put his bag down with ours, and I thought, how nice, we will have lunch together. But no. He waited to see that we were getting a table and attention from the waiters, and off he went to eat in the Chinese dining room.

The room was filled with Japanese tourists eating and drinking with their usual gusto. We were given a small table by an open window. Lunch was delicious and served by a nice man who was upset that we didn't eat everything: seven different dishes, rice, two soups, and melon!!

When we arrived here, Mr. An Wei met us. He will be our local Xi'an guide. He knows a lot about contemporary American literature and seems to have read a lot. It is not clear where and how he has found books. He got more suggestions and names of authors from H. He talks about Hans Brinker, all of E. B. White's children's books, and Laura Ingals Wilder. Amazing!

We had about a fifteen-minute "rest" as they say, and set off in a car to see the much publicized clay figures that were discovered in 1974 20 miles (30 kilometers) east of Xi'an. Our driver was the absolute opposite of all the other Chinese drivers we have ever had. He drove so slowly it took about one-and-a-half hours to do what we could have done in about a half hour. I found myself longing for the reckless speed demons of Ürümqi. But when we finally got to the spot and saw the figures, it was more than worth it. The road was crowded with trucks and carts pulled by donkeys, mules, horses, and even by people. Thousands of bicycle riders and many people walking.

Qin Shi Huang was a statesman of the rising landlord class in ancient China. By conquering surrounding states he ended the struggle of the Warring States and founded in 221 B.C. the first multinational feudal state in China's history. He instituted unified local administrations, made private ownership by landlords and farmers legal, and unified laws. His tomb is a large burial mound some distance from the huge army vault that houses the clay figures. It reputedly took eleven years to build and was started the year he unified the states. The mound is nowhere near as high and wide as it was when it was built, the result of 2,000 years of erosion, natural causes, and human destruction. We can't figure out if the tomb has ever been opened, if everything has been destroyed, or what the status is. There are records describing the interior. We walked up the path leading to the tomb's closed gate and saw the chart depicting palaces, a ceiling symbolizing stars made of pearls, and a physical map of China that covered the floor and had mercury flowing in the rivers.

It had been the custom when an emperor or king died, to put with him in his tomb all the things he would need in the next world; food, clothing, grain, cooking and eating utensils, gold, jewels, as well as animals, servants, and soldiers, who were buried alive. This enlightened man, Qin Shi Huang, instead, had life-size figures made of clay and it is estimated that as many as 6,000 figures were buried in groups to defend his tomb. The story is that a rival king who hated Qin broke into this vault after Qin died, stole all the weapons, smashed many of the figures, and set the place on fire. This accounts for the statues in the display cases that are black.

The Chinese say this remarkable find was "stumbled upon" in 1974, and we have been told that it was found by workers digging for an irrigation project.

A museum around a courtyard has been built with rooms for exhibits, and a huge dome has been erected over the entire vault site so that it will not be damaged by weather and the archeological work can go on undisturbed. In one exhibit hall there are representative statues. They are blackened by fire and obviously pieced together and mended. In other rooms are examples of armor, weapons, and objects of daily use. Inside the vault a platform has been erected around the whole area so that visitors can look down from the sides on this remarkable sight. A bridge crosses over from one side to the other so that you can see from all angles. Even though I have seen the statues that were in the exhibit at the Metropolitan Museum in New York last year, I wasn't prepared for what lay before me. Row after row of soldiers and horses seemed to be slowly marching out of the earth. Only a small area has been dug out, and only a few statues are whole. These are lined up in straight formation. Down in the pit are many workers, mostly women, who seemed to be just sitting around the way Chinese workers often seem to be in factories. But in reality, they were painstakingly dusting off fragments, putting them together, reassembling this 2,000-year-old army.

We had dinner with Mr. Bai Yu-fung, the deputy director of the Foreign Office of Shanxi Province. He is a terribly nice man and used to work for the *People's Daily*. He took us to a public restaurant, where we ate the most delicious dinner upstairs. He said he was trying out this restaurant to see if it would be suitable for tourists. The cook came out to see us, and we told them it was much more than suitable. It was perfect in every respect.

Thursday, August 14
Xi'an

THIS MORNING we got up at 6:30. At breakfast we sat with an American who had been teaching in a university here for the past year. His wife was with him, and they were enjoying a trip around the country before going home. He told us that when he went out to see the clay figures on the same road we took, he saw a Chinese woman walking along in the middle of the trucks, wagons, and bicycles, naked as on the day she was born. He couldn't believe his eyes and tried to call his guide's attention to this strange sight. But the guide looked straight ahead, not answering. When they had gone some distance, the man turned to him and said, "If you did see a naked woman back there, she was crazy." Nothing more was said. The people who were near the woman on the road never looked at her, the teacher added. It was as if she were not there.

This reminds me of the woman we saw in Beijing. We came out of a photo library one afternoon and a large, sloppily dressed gray-haired Chinese woman was leaning on our car, waving her arms and shouting, "I have seen God, I have seen God. I will go to Heaven." Everyone with us was upset and didn't know what to do. H. said she was just like so many "bag" ladies in New York, it didn't seem strange to us at all and we were not afraid of her. Finally someone persuaded her to leave us. It interests me that there were no police or revolutionary committee people around to take care of either of these situations, and that crazy people are acknowledged, if reluctantly. On our other visits nothing like these episodes ever would have happened.

The American teacher said that the students he had taught were for the most part apolitical. They have been told so many different things in the last few years that they don't believe or don't give a damn about anything anymore. He also said that the Chinese authorities didn't like him to be alone with or get too friendly with people. He felt this was not so much because of what he'd say to them that might corrupt them, but that someone might tell him things the authorities would prefer he did not know. It's true that most Chinese people we've talked to seem quite willing to tell all about their problems in the Cultural Revolution, with the Gang of Four, and their humiliations, persecutions, and struggles, though we never ask for details.

He told us that the bureaucracy and red tape were so thick that students could never get books from the university library. He took them out himself for his students.

Our first visit was to the big mosque, which is gorgeous in the arrangement of buildings. It is old, classical Chinese architecture and being restored at government expense. Fundamentally it is beautiful and it was nice walking from one courtyard to the next, over little bridges and by fountains. But there are always these incongruous touches in even the most beautiful places; a bunch of towels thrown on a shrub, an enamel spitton next to a heavenly carved chair (better than spitting on the floor, though), laundry hanging outside all the doorways. However, it was swept and clean. The huge worship hall needs a lot of work. The ceiling is lovely but seems to be collapsing and much in need of paint. There are mounds and heaps of earth and bricks, stones and old tile and pieces of carving, debris from old palaces and temples, all in heaps. Inside the building on one side is a roped-off area absolutely crammed with old furniture.

The imam wore a white jacket and a close-fitting round white hat and looked like a doctor or an important chef. While he told us some things about this mosque, we sat in a pretty open room and had tea out of tiny cups with covers. He put the cover on his cup after every sip. The furniture was teak or dark mahogany inlaid with mother-of-pearl, rich and luxurious. I remember seeing the same kind of chairs and tables in the reception room of a blanket factory outside Beijing on one of our other visits and wondering where it came from. Now I have a good idea.

This mosque was closed for one year during the Cultural Revolution; the imam went to the country. He has been at this mosque for seventeen years and has made the big trek to Mecca. Now the state gives the Mosque money, it owns some houses, which are rented (church landlord!), and it gets voluntary contributions from Muslim believers, of whom there are 30,000 in Xi'an, he said.

This is such a different story from 1972, or even 1977. It's hard to take in. There were no believers in those years, so we were told. No one believed in all that superstitious stuff. It is clear that religion is important to some people, especially the minority groups, and that the Chinese government is making it possible for them to practice their beliefs.

We then drove out to the museum, which used to be a Confucian shrine. It is a beautiful set of buildings and has some wonderful things from the old palace. The clay figures buried in tombs were made smaller instead of life size, being merely symbolic of what the emperors and kings would need in their next life. At this museum they have over 3,000 of these small figures, and about 800 are on exhibit. A few still have color here and there. Imagine what must be under the ground, here in Xi'an especially, as it was the capital of eleven dynasties from the eleventh century B.C. to the early tenth century A.D. It was also the starting point of the old Silk Road. Of course, a lot has been dug up, a lot stolen. "There has been much plundering," we were told.

To a nice restaurant for lunch, where we were the only people. Everyone else had been cleared out, as is the custom in many restaurants we're taken to, and often in dining cars on trains. I believe it is considered polite to visitors and should make us feel special. It makes me feel uncomfortable and conspicuous, but it doesn't happen as often as it used to, thank goodness.

I was led to the WC by one of the waitresses, across a big courtyard, up a flight of steps, and down a long hall with rooms on each side. Many Chinese were either visiting or living there. When I emerged from the toilet, one or two heads were poking out of every door, so I smiled and bowed, first on one side and then on the other, saying "Neehow" (hello), and everyone smiled and bowed back.

Still Thursday, August 14
Chengdu

WE FLEW HERE, in a cargo plane again. It is interesting flying that way for a change but not very comfortable and very hard to read or look out the windows. We are in another huge Russian-built hotel with air conditioning. We had dinner quickly by ourselves and met with the governor of the province, a nice man who looked as if he

89

had had a pretty tough time. He had only one arm and seemed battle-scarred to me. But there was no talk about anything personal, or even the Cultural Revolution or Gang of Four, only about economics and the new experiments that have been tried in this province.

The general idea is to give a factory or enterprise some control in management. For example, say a factory can turn out one hundred gadgets in a given time. Under this plan they produce 80 percent for the government and produce what they want with the 20 percent capacity left. In other words, they are given control over how they use some of their capacity. They can produce, and market this 20 percent any way they want; they don't have to sell it to the government. And they can invest the profit any way they choose. It gives them a chance to experiment a little and to be a tiny bit independent of the overall planning. It seems to have worked very well, and people talk about it a lot—the Sichuan economic experiment.

Friday, August 15
Chengdu

RIGHT AFTER BREAKFAST we set off for the temple erected on the site of the thatched hut lived in by Du Fu, the famous poet. He lived there for four years in the eighth century. The temple was built during the Song Dynasty, A.D. 960–1280. It is utterly beautiful and like the mosque yesterday; classical Chinese architecture with paths over bridges and pools, flowers, lovely open rooms, and wonderful tiled roofs. There is a collection of his poems and scrolls and several statues. And an assortment of varying and beautiful calligraphy. The Temple Gongbuci is especially dedicated to the poet and houses the poems.

From there to a silver-filigree factory where a most boring manager talked to us, afterward taking us to several work rooms. We watched women (there were only one or two men in each room, compared with about fifteen women) going through the stages of making filigree vases from silver wire. Everything was done by hand, no machinery except two or three things that wound the wire onto spools, but this was being turned by hand. The women had blower pedals they worked by foot, and small welding torches run by gasoline in open containers. Very primitive, and dangerous, I would think. The gasoline could so easily catch fire from the torches. The manager told us that an American firm had ordered 4,000 small vases, and he said each one takes twelve days to produce. I figure he meant that there is a waiting time for drying or melding together between steps in the making of a vase. It appeared that each woman was doing the same thing to many vases, then sending them on to the next worker who did something else. So though it may take twelve days to complete a vase, a considerable number will be finished at the same time.

Most of the things are too gaudy for my taste and are terribly expensive.

Then we went to an exhibition hall, where everything was more or less the same. The brocade was pretty and there were some nice old simple designs. I always would buy material, but we have enough and our bags are already too heavy. Also, everything costs so much I don't feel like buying anything.

From there to the public food market; it was wonderful. Every known kind of vegetable, flower, plant, fruit, eggs, meat. We bought a huge pear that weighed one-half kilo, which is one pound and one ounce, and ate it before lunch. First I scrubbed it with soap and the nailbrush, then peeled it. It was delicious. I wonder why we can't, or don't, grow fruit like that: crisp and juicy.

The poor chickens were all tied up and looked so sad. They are bought alive and carried home by the legs with their heads hanging down. Skinned rabbits with their heads still on were lined up on a bench. I wonder sometimes how I can ever eat meat.

After lunch Li came and told us there have been floods in Tibet and Nepal, the road and bridges are washed out, so we won't be able to exit that way, as we had hoped. It's a big disappointment but having been in floods in Sikkim, I can believe the conditions. So we have decided to come back here after visiting Lhasa, fly to Shanghai and from there to Hong Kong. We think there are planes for that schedule, but it will probably turn out they only fly once a week. When Li first came in, he said, "Bad news about Tibet," I thought he was going to say we couldn't go at all. We know the Chinese are not anxious for us to go. They talk about the altitude as if it were a devil or curse that no one can conquer, and they constantly mention our age.

A group of Tibetan men and women are in this hotel and have been to Beijing. The women are dressed in their own style clothes, a long, full, coatlike dress usually dark brown or black or gray, over a blouse, and an apron. They wear a jacket if it's cold. Men wear a coat that is like the Mongolian *dal*, almost like an old Chinese coat that pulls around and fastens on the shoulder and the side, big boots and big hats. They are very genial, but they looked dirty and travel worn. A tiny, neat, clean Chinese woman is accompanying them.

Harrison went to a steel mill, but I enjoyed an afternoon off and had a nice nap. He had a good time at the factory. The management people told him about all the troubles they have now with the young people. They don't care about anything, don't want to work, have bad fights among themselves. It is the same story we heard from the American teacher in Xi'an.

The weather is gray and overcast and not too hot: fine for us but bad for the rice crop, which won't ripen unless the sun comes out. The crops look wonderful, however; agriculture is the number-one production in this area. Cucumbers and squash are grown on trellises like grapes.

Tonight we had dinner with the head of the Foreign Office of Sichuan Province, a man who looks as if he had had a hard life, and he has. He was a soldier until Liberation and has lived here ever since. He was in trouble during the Cultural Revolution, said he was "struggled with." Then he looked across the table at the young man who is our local companion and said, "He was struggled with, too, because his parents were in trouble." I asked him what happened to his parents, and he said, "My mother died in the Cultural Revolution. She committed suicide." I was shocked at myself for asking, and once more it came home so clearly how many terrible things happened in this country in those years.

We learned later that his father was a follower of Liu Schao-chi (the first-named successor to Mao who died in jail but has been reinstated posthumously) and was in the government. His mother was put in prison and tortured. She jumped from a fourth-story window but did not die;

she was taken home and died there. His brother was beaten to death. He was also beaten but somehow survived. He has many scars on his face.

Saturday, August 16
Chengdu

THIS MORNING we went first to the local newspaper office and had an interesting time with the editors. People are so honest now compared with what they used to be, very frank about what happened to them personally and about the damage to everything in the Cultural Revolution and the troubles caused by the Gang of Four. I think all the older men we've seen had a bad time. The editors at this paper lost their jobs, spent the ten years cleaning floors, explaining their "errors," and working down on the pig farms. Harrison said today he guessed there were a lot of pig farming experts in the room, and the editors laughed and replied, "Not experts, but we certainly learned the ABC's of taking care of pigs."

This paper was not shut down but was managed by allies of the Gang. Papers were a valuable tool for spreading news the way they wanted it told, and for propaganda. The Gang had control of the *People's Daily*, and if this paper had anything different from what came out of Beijing, it was attacked. At present they print the *People's Daily*, which is telephotoed from Beijing, other local newspapers besides their own, and some magazines.

Harrison asked how many people were killed in

Chengdu during the Cultural Revolution, and they answered that there was fighting in every institution and several thousand people were killed. But they felt more were killed in other places.

From there we went to a cotton factory where everything is done from making the thread to dying and printing the fabric. Our guide thinks the designs are too bright, that they appeal only to simple country people. But I think, on the whole, they are pretty and much better than what we've seen on earlier visits.

Back at the hotel we had a delicious lunch, a very short rest, and on to the Temple Wu Hou-si. This is dedicated to the memory of the scholar and strategist, Zhu Geliang. He lived from A.D. 181 to 234 and is one of the chief heroes of the *Romance of the Three Kingdoms*, a well-known historical novel, and several plays.

After the shrine we visited Sichuan Medical College. It was started in 1910 with American, British, and German help and called West China Union University. According to the folder, "It was in 1952 in which year readjustments of institutions of higher education across the country were made, that Sichuan Medical College took its present name."

The director met us and talked to us in the reception room. Harrison had asked to talk to some doctors, but none turned up. The only interesting thing, to me, that the director said was when I asked about mental illness. He answered, "We have many cases." On previous visits we were told that there was no place for neurosis, let alone psychosis, in a socialist society, and that there was no mental illness and no mental hospitals.

At the end of our tour around the hospital buildings we were confronted by a woman with a stethoscope and told we should have our blood pressure taken, which would cost 5 *yuan* each, to see if we are fit for Tibet. Before that was accomplished, they said it had been arranged at another hospital for us to have complete physical examinations with cardiograms, X rays of our insides, blood tests, and other details. That would cost us 25 *yuan* each, about $17. At that I blew my top. Harrison had already blown his, and I thought his blood pressure would be well over 300. It was so irritating, and obviously so unplanned and helter-skelter, to think of being examined by strange doctors, going from here to there, with no one really in charge. I wasn't going to submit to it, and neither was H. We had complete physical exams in New York, had letters from our doctors, had both lived in high altitudes, and were used to it. As I have written before, the Chinese are terrified of the high altitude in Tibet. Lhasa is 12,000 feet, and they act as if it were the most dangerous place in the world to go. Maybe they are afraid of it for other reasons.

We finally decided to have heart and blood pressure checks, and if there was anything wrong or worrisome, we could have more tests. H. was first, and the doctor tentatively listened to his heart for a long time, then took his blood pressure, which was 170 over 80, just right for his age. She wasn't happy about the pulse, so she called for another doctor who went all over H. again. Neither doctor asked him to take off his shirt; they just undid several buttons and put the stethoscope inside. They thought he might have a murmur until he told them he had a pacemaker. Neither had detected it, and I am not sure they knew what it was. It makes a different kind of pulse at times, or rather sometimes there is a double beat. I have never understood it, only regard it as a modern miracle.

My blood pressure was 120 over 70, just the same as

Li's, and they worried that it is too low for an American!!
I guess that is all we have to go through.

After dinner we went to the movies to see *Love and
Legacy*, a new film made this year by the Xi'an Film
Company. It was about a widowed doctor and his two
children, the good girl doctor and the bad boy
photographer. It was simple, yet touching and honest. It
showed the Red Guards rampaging around the country
and doing senseless damage in the Cultural Revolution,
but it showed no cruelty. The father was portrayed as too
exacting and narrow, wanting his children only to work
and study. It was a story of good and bad, and good won
in the end, and the father realized he had expected too
much from his children and hadn't given them the love
and attention they needed.

The acting was natural, the photography good, and Li
said it was full of real China-isms. The peasant family
was depicted as healthy and living well; the doctor, an
intellectual, had a nice house, a car, and a driver. The
girl was lovely and an excellent actress, as was the sup-
porting cast.

Sunday, August 17
Chengdu

THIS MORNING we drove out to a commune. Unfortunately it was raining and very muddy, so we
couldn't walk around much. We had the usual "briefing"
by a woman who is the deputy head of the brigade. The

head is a man. There are no women heads of communes, we were told. This woman's husband is in her brigade, and she says he doesn't mind her being the deputy; he recognizes it as a "fair division of labor." They have two children, twelve and ten, and share the housework.

We saw a typical peasant country house, built around a little court with the kitchen in one room; pigs, including a sow with fourteen new piglets next to her, in their pens; and rooms for sleeping and living on the other sides. Probably more than one family is housed here, since there were three older women standing around, all knitting.

The pig manure is pushed into a pit under the pen; the human excreta goes into the same place, and from that comes a gas, which is called bio gas. It is piped to the stove in the kitchen and used in cooking. Fantastic, but pretty smelly.

I know that in the United States some people are showing interest in energy from manure. I have seen several articles in farm and garden magazines, and the farmer who lives near us in the country has been reading up on it. He says many others are, too. From his cow manure he could make enough energy to power the milking machines and have plenty left for fertilizer. It certainly makes more sense than our present energy policy, being dependent on substances that are getting more and more expensive, that are diminishing and may run out completely.

We looked at the commune store, which had such simple necessary items as toothpaste, cooking pots, towels, and some nice straw hats and baskets. I bought a little set of five baskets, all fitting into each other, very well made and pretty.

Just before lunch we walked around in a park with lots

of lotus and wonderful flowers and a wisteria vine that must be centuries old. It was like an enormous marble snake coming out of the ground.

The painter who did the horse scrolls and pictures that I like so much is Xu Bei-hong. He painted in the early 1950s, right after Liberation. Another painter, Chang Da-qiax, has pictures hanging in Chengdu, but he lives in Taiwan. Formerly this would not have been mentioned; in fact his pictures would not have been shown. *Taiwan* was, and still is more or less, a dirty word.

Lunch was at a pleasant place with a spotless ladies' room and a lock on the door. After lunch I visited it again, but this time there was no water.

At lunch Li and our local guide ordered a bottle of red wine because I said I liked it. They brought what was left home. It's quite good, not as sweet as the banquet red wine. I gave Li the vermouth I bought, which is heavy and bitter, and I thought it might exacerbate the hives that have appeared due to the antibiotic pills I've been taking.

After lunch we went to the Baoguangsi, or Precious Light Monastery. It is also known as the Divine Light or Heavenly Light Monastery, depending on what book you look in or whom you ask. Most things seem to have several names, all enough alike so you can tell what people are referring to. This monastery was founded during the Tang Dynasty, A.D. 618–907. About thirty monks live and practice their religion here, chanting Buddhist prayers night and morning. It is a huge monastery and includes Lohan Hall in which there is a collection of more than five hundred statues. It could be quite beautiful, but it was dusty and dirty and generally a mess. It was full of people who pushed and crowded around us and spat on the ground.

This evening we went to the local opera, which is much more relaxed and amusing than the Peking Opera, or any other we've seen here. It was the story of a girl whose fiancé died before the marriage, but her in-laws made her go through with the ceremony and treated her as their son's widow and therefore their property. All this was long ago, naturally; part of the awful business of people owning other people. The opera opens with her in mourning dress on the one-hundredth day since her marriage to a "straw man." Her maid or companion urged her to take off the dress and stop being in mourning. She did and ran home to her parents, who, though they agreed with her in-laws, felt sorry for her and allowed her to stay. She fell in love with an eminent scholar who wanted to marry her. But her family forbade it, saying she was a widow; widows never married again, and she should return to her in-laws, where she belonged.

So she and the scholar ran away and, with the help of her companion and his servant, managed a restaurant and bar. They were successful, and their fame spread far and wide. Both families learned of their whereabouts and appeared, intending to drag the girl off. But true love triumphed in the end; the parents and in-laws relented and gave them permission to marry and everyone was happy.

The costumes were gorgeous, the sets elaborate, the audience adored it and obviously knew it by heart. None of these operas was shown during the Cultural Revolution or the days of the Gang. What did these people who so clearly cherish their operas think when they were forbidden? Did they swallow the line that they were bourgeois? What does that really mean, anyway? I get very tired of slogans, and the Chinese are high on them.

The way the audience looks compared with the actors on the stage is such a contrast it is hard to believe. The audience wears the usual shirts and pants—no one wears skirts out here—and if it's hot, the men just wear those sleeveless undershirts that look like mens' old-fashioned bathing suits, in green, red, or blue, sometimes whitish. Not like a Metropolitan Opera audience, though even there men wear blue jeans sometimes—to show off, I think. I remember not too long ago that if a man didn't have a tie, he was not allowed in the door.

Monday, August 18
Chengdu

THIS MORNING we went out—a two-hour drive—to see what we were told is the Dujiangyan irrigation system. The geography book put out by the Foreign Language Press in Beijing calls it the Tukiang Dam system and says that in 250 B.C. "the people cut a breach-proof rock walled course through the mountain." The Nagel guidebook to China refers to it as the Guan xian Dam and adds that in 250 B.C. "the scholar Li Bing had an opening made in a wall of rock and created this remarkable system of dams and embankments, and that his son carried on the work after him.

Whatever, it is a thrilling sight, especially when you think it has been functioning for over two thousand years—twenty centuries compared with the United States' not quite four. It is a system of water diverted into

101

canals and streams with new dams and locks. It is pretty remarkable, and after what we've been through, it is wonderful to see and hear rushing water. The geography book goes on to say, "Altogether the people built two thousand dikes and ten trunk and five hundred twenty branch canals totalling one thousand one hundred sixty five kilometers." This made possible natural irrigation for over 3 million *mu* (about 500,000 acres or 200,000 hectares) and made the Chengdu plain a rich agricultural area. The dikes were made entirely of woven bamboo baskets filled with rocks. The book says the same method is used today because the materials are handy and "the result is both economical and durable." Before 1949 it fell into disrepair but, we were told, the Communist Party has repaired and expanded it so that now it serves 7 million *mu*, which is about 1.2 million acres (50,000 hectares). It is the richest agricultural region in China. Three crops a year of rice, sugar cane, tobacco, rape seed, and so on, are normal.

We climbed up a square wooden tower with open balconies on each landing and got a good view of the river rushing down, filled with logs from the mountain forests. We could see the locks that govern where the water goes. Just above the system are temples built into the side of the mountain. We drove up to a lookout to see the whole system from another angle, then walked down the hill through the various temples. Though they are intrinsically beautiful, everything is so grubby. The ground is covered with Popsicle papers and sticks, sunflower seeds and shells, and there was not a trash basket anywhere.

We walked across the river and back on a long suspension bridge that swayed over the torrent. Here and there were holes in the slats and it would have been easy to trip and fall, not all the way into the water, but maybe to get a foot stuck. Anyway, I don't enjoy heights and this was, or seemed, quite high above the water. It is good to have new experiences, but I was glad to get back on the ground.

We had lunch in a guest house nearby. Our host was the local head of the Foreign Office. We had some peach liquor, more like a liqueur than a wine. It is made in this area and is awfully good, a million times better than Mao Tai, at least to me. Our host drank at least three "Gambey's" (bottoms up) and made a lot of toasts to us.

In the afternoon Harrison went to the university, but I stayed in and washed my hair and did my nails. I don't use any polish on my fingernails here but have kept my toes bright red. It makes me feel nice, and I love to see the expressions on Chinese faces when they look at my feet where the red shows through socks or stockings and sandals.

H. told me about his visit to Chengdu University. Originally it was a teacher's college, founded in 1905 by missionaries. Now it is a regular university. The rest of what he had to report is not a pretty story.

Though it was closed for six years during the Cultural Revolution, there was a great deal of physical fighting. Seven hundred students were involved. One hundred were killed, 200 wounded or disabled. The dean of biology died. A lecturer was beaten to death. Twenty-eight faculty members were tortured to death, died of their wounds, or committed suicide.

Every kind of weapon was used; heavy and light machine guns, submachine guns, antiaircraft guns, cannons, automatic rifles, and hand grenades. That period is referred to as the Time of Terror.

For the last three years restoration has been going on.

103

Now teaching is normal. Students are accepted according to their scores on exams, professors have been reinstated. The university at present has 3,000 students, and in 1981 it will admit 1,000 more. There are 115 full-time professors.

The members of the faculty who were cohorts of the Gang are still there. Those opposing the Gang, who were put in jail or sent to pig farms or otherwise tormented, are there, too. The head man said to H. that people on both sides "apparently" get along on the surface, but underneath they harbor deep resentment. "It's no easy job running a university these days," he said.

Tuesday, August 19, 9 A.M.
On the plane to Lhasa

UP AT 5:30, breakfast at the airport, where we met the American Chinese geologist who, with his Swiss wife, sat at the next table to us in the dining room at Chengdu. She has gone back to Beijing, from where she will return to Zurich, where they live. He is on his way to Shanghai to see his father, who lives there. He teaches in Zurich but does a lot of traveling in Europe as well as China, advising and helping in his field.

I don't know how I feel about Tibet. For many years I was longing to go. I read everything I could and fell in love with the idea of a romantic people living in this remote, beautiful country that so few foreigners had ever seen. What I have read in the past few years has been

104

mostly out-and-out propaganda from the Chinese side and reports and stories by Tibetans who had to flee to India and who now are refugees living in many countries, including the United States. But since there has been so much fighting and so much destruction of the real Tibetan culture (savage and backward as it was, it was theirs and they weren't trying to force it on any other country) and so much Chinese influence, I don't really want to see it. I'm afraid it will be depressing the way Mongolia and Inner Mongolia are to me, a country and its people forced to live under the authority of another foreign government. The Chinese have made many changes; freeing slaves, establishing schools, and, they say, providing medical care for everyone. But the Tibetans might have done all this in their own way if they'd been left alone.

The fact that we can't go out and home through Nepal is a bitter blow. I hate the idea of going back to Chengdu, then on to another city, the same old routine for several days more.

We are flying over mountains that look as if they went on forever. Most are snow-covered, some are dark underneath. Exciting, mysterious, scary.

Same day, after dinner at the guest house, Lhasa

WE ARRIVED AT about 10:00 this morning. All of China is on the same time as Beijing no matter how many time zones away. In Tibet it was actually 8:00 according to the sun.

Coming down from cruising height we flew over several heavenly green valleys and then followed a river with bare stone mountains on one side. We flew awfully close to them, down the valley to where it looked as if two rivers met, then turned and flew back the other side of the stone mountain to the airport.

Our first breath of Tibetan air was wonderful. So many places, including here, remind Harrison of Montana. I am thinking of Colorado, where I lived for a while during World War II. The same kind of thin, clear, cool air and bright blue sky with such white clouds.

There were lots of Chinese army people at the airport, and a nice little Chinese woman who will be our local guide greeted us. We made the trip here in a Toyota Land Cruiser over a bumpy road that followed the curving river. The airport, which is on a military post, is 75 miles (120 kilometers) away. The Chinese never expected to have tourists in Tibet. Li keeps saying, "Only special people are allowed to come here." Lindblad began running a few tours from Hong Kong to Lhasa just this summer, and there are some French people staying in this guest house. We were told that there are plans to build another airport nearer the city.

Compared with traffic on Chinese roads, there wasn't much. Some trucks and jeeps, mostly army; a few tractors pulling carts and trailers; very few horse- or animal-drawn carts; several Tibetans thumbing a ride. No riders on horses, which surprised us. Whenever a truck appeared ahead of us, our driver got right up behind it, and, since the road is narrow, we often couldn't pass for a long time. I can't describe the dust. Just as bad as in the desert. At one corner a huge painted Buddha is carved in the rock. First sign of what this country used to be all about.

We stopped for the obvious reason along the road, and our tiny guide and I squatted down beside each other in a typical three-hole Chinese outhouse with waist-high par-

106

titions between the holes, above which my head always sticks up. I will only say the stench was unbelievable, here in the high, clear, clean mountain air, and when I emerged, I swayed a bit. Our little guide grabbed my arm thinking I was giddy from the altitude, but she was wrong. It was the smell.

From quite far away we began to see the Potala, the palace that, according to old legends, was built in the seventh century A.D. by King Songtsen Gampo when he married two princesses, one Chinese, the other from Nepal. According to the tales he built this huge castle over a fortress that was on Red Hill, a high rocky mass that rose up out of the valley. At first the Potala looked small to us, a strange illusion when you realize it is nearly one thousand feet from the valley floor, and more in length, has thirteen stories and even originally had 999 rooms. The Potala today is the palace that was restored and enlarged by the fifth Dalai Lama in the seventeenth century.

As we got closer, we could see the colors: the gold roofs, the red below, and the gray-white below that. But, oh dear, how the Chinese have spoiled the approach. Oil storage tanks, electric light poles and wires, lumber and coal yards, and construction sites clutter the landscape, and at the foot of the Potala in the city is a big complex of Chinese buildings.

We are in a guest house and have a suite, a bedroom separated from a sitting room by heavy red velvet curtains, and a bathroom, up one flight. The beds are comfortable and nicely made, and the living room has a sofa, three big armchairs, a desk, and a big closet for clothes. I definitely feel the altitude, feel giddy and weak in the knees when I come up the stairs. We have two large canvas bags of oxygen in case we need them.

A man we met at lunch told us that the poverty and

disease here are beyond description. Goiters, eye troubles, cripples, and beggars. I noticed that the children who crowded around us in the courtyard were covered with what looks like impetigo, and they are filthy. But underneath that exterior, they are good-looking children and very friendly. They chew bubble gum, great pink and gray globs protruding from their grimy little faces.

Everyone thought we should take it easy or go to bed for the rest of the day, but we had only a short nap then strolled around the courtyard to get our altitude legs, so to speak. It is much warmer outdoors than in. Trees are planted right next to the building, so the sun is kept out.

At 5:00 we went to see the Nepalese consul general to talk about the chances of our getting to Nepal. He said the road on the Nepal side is all repaired and that mail and buses are coming through. Harrison is so tactful that when we got back to the guest house, he just told Li that the Nepal road is all fixed, the king and queen are waiting to receive us, and our ambassador expects us for a visit. I think the Chinese have never wanted us to leave by that route, though they are letting us go to Shigatse, only 200 miles (300 kilometers) from Nepal, so I can't see why not. There's nothing on that border they want to hide, and we will have seen all the dirt and poverty and lack of success in their trying to make the Tibetans the way they want them by the time we get to the last stop. It is just their bureaucratic stubbornness and intransigence. I would never have been as gentle as H. I would have blurted out that we know they are making excuses, the bridge was never washed out, there was only a landslide that people are already walking over, and what's the matter with the Chinese that they can't fix their road when the Nepalese have already repaired theirs. But that kind of approach doesn't usually work.

108

It was pleasant visiting the Nepalese. He is a very nice, genial man, and he and his wife live in a pretty house inside a compound with other Nepalese families. They are the only country represented here and have had a consulate in Lhasa for 146 years. We had a glass of tea, English tea with milk, though they call it "Nepalese tea." Madame came in, pretty with a diamond in her nose and a red mark on her forehead. She speaks English and Chinese, no Tibetan. They are the only foreigners living here, five Nepalese families in the compound. She hates it, says it's difficult to get anything, there is nothing to do, they can't wait to leave. They've been here nearly two years. It is considered a hardship post. The winters are awful. She knits a lot.

The consul general will contact people for us in Katmandu if we can get the Chinese moving.

At supper we sat with a Hong Kong photographer who is here, being paid by the Chinese to do a picture book about Tibet, and they won't let him go anywhere that ordinary tourists don't go. He is pleasant and amusing. His companions are all sick, fainting and throwing up from the altitude. He asked H. how old he is and when H. said "seventy-one," his mouth opened wide in shock. He couldn't imagine such an age, or for such old people to be in Tibet, let alone feeling all right.

We saw a Chinese documentary of Tibet called *The Roof of the World*. It was made in 1978. Except for a few lovely pictures of scenery, flowers, birds, and animals, it was terribly dull: mostly Chinese people taking the temperature of the water at a hot springs; Chinese climbing mountains; Chinese growing vegetables; Chinese discovering oil; Chinese discovering minerals in the hills. There was scarcely a Tibetan in it.

A Lindblad group of about twenty-five tourists is staying at a guest house outside the city, and the film was

109

shown there. The audience consisted of them, us, our guides, and many Tibetans and Chinese of all ages. As in many Chinese theaters, the audience talked all the time and made a lot of noise.

Wednesday, August 20
Lhasa

LI DIDN'T feel well today. He took some tranquilizers and went with H. to the museum, but he clearly felt lousy. I didn't sleep at all, or that's the way it seemed, and I didn't feel too sharp either, so decided to skip the exhibit of tortures.

The museum consists mostly of a collection of torture practices of the old Tibetan society, and they are pretty gruesome, Harrison reported. Skin, skulls, amputated hands and feet; the remains of children who were skinned (flayed) alive; the remains of a girl who with her two sisters and her mother were roasted alive because they were believed to be children of the devil—this measure was the only way to save them from many hells. But worse than any of those, H. said, were the sculptured clay figures in a series called the Wrath of the Serfs. In the most realistic way they showed the punishments, tortures, and cruel customs and rites inflicted by the rich on the poor, by landowners on serfs. Unbelievable. The figures have actual clothes, chains and whips to add to the realistic portrayal of these evil doings. Serfs stagger under heavy loads of grain and goods for the landlord;

serfs are being beaten and dragged to jail; a baby cries from hunger while his mother grinds meal with the little strength she has left; a woman is tied to a stake and her heart will be torn out while she is alive; a monk is pushing a struggling little boy into a box to be buried alive in the cornerstone of a monastery; a man with spikes driven under his fingernails is strapped to an ox and sent out to die. People are being beaten and jabbed and children cry—Harrison said he could almost hear them. And along with all this a photo of Lowell Thomas and his son having dinner.

I think the Chinese overdo the propaganda about how cruel the Tibetans were without remembering that they have been guilty of terrible crimes against human beings themselves, and, in recent years, without the excuse of

Three Tibetan girls

superstition. I wonder if someday there might be a museum here depicting all the horrors and destruction of the Cultural Revolution, of what the Chinese and Red Guards inflicted on the Tibetans.

Before lunch we walked in the Chinese section of Lhasa. We visited the department store, which I thought was pretty well stocked and like any other I've seen in an outpost city. Harrison thought it was "low level." There were some nice pots and bowls and lots of wristwatches. I was surprised at the prices, more than I know Li makes in a month. I said I didn't see who could afford them, and with a trace of bitterness, he replied, "People get paid well for serving out here. Salaries are much higher than in Beijing."

We strolled in the park at the foot of the Potala and took some pictures. It is a very weird place, really spooky, and I can imagine all sorts of terrible things being plotted and carried out in those dark inside rooms, all in the name of Buddha.

After lunch and a nap we walked to and around the old town. The poverty is appalling, and a lot of the Tibetans look as if they had some terrible disease, and they are *so* dirty. Someone told me they take a bath once a year, but I doubt the people we saw today do even that. In *To Lhasa in Disguise*, written by William McGovern in 1924, I read, "Most Tibetans never touch their bodies with water during the whole course of their lives and become practically incased in a layer of fat and dirt which serves the useful function of keeping out the cold." And in another place he describes Tibet as "a paradise of filth."

Many women carry prayer beads like rosaries. Men, women, and children have prayer wheels. (A little round box with a wheel that goes around in the wind as you move, at the end of a handle about 12 inches [30 centimeters] long.) There are prayer flags everywhere, hanging on posts, on trees and bushes, on strings, and draped all over a statue outside the Jokhang Monastery in the middle of the city. They are just as they were in Sikkim, raggedy pieces of material, generally gray but sometimes colored. Prayers are written on them, and when the wind blows, the prayers are carried to the gods.

When we go out, we are accosted every few seconds by Tibetans who have something to sell: beads, jewelry, silver buckles, knives, bowls—you name it. Our Hong Kong photographer friend bought a beautiful knife in a carved silver case for one of the Frenchwomen who is in a group staying in this guest house. He paid 80 *yuan*, roughly $60. Most things offered us look new and cheap, but even if we see something wonderful, I don't want to do that sort of buying from beggars anywhere, especially here. I am amazed the Chinese allow it, but they almost encourage it. These poor people come right up to the steps of the guest house, and no one stops them, even though there is a high wall surrounding the guest house compound and a big iron gate with a gatekeeper.

We visited a carpet factory housed in a dilapidated, cluttered building with a dirt floor. Women and girls sit in front of the looms and weave by hand, just as they do in China, Mongolia, in any rug factory we have visited. The rugs are not as handsome as those we used to get from Sikkim. Those rugs were bright-colored and had dragons and interesting designs. These designs and colors are dull in comparison. That seems strange because the Sikkim rugs were copied from Tibet. I remember the Tibetan man who was teaching the Sikkimese how to make them. He was tall and handsome and wore one turquoise earring.

From the factory we went to the house of a model worker, a woman who won a medal for a rug she wove that is now in the Mao Mausoleum in Beijing. We walked through back alleys, picking our way through litter and dirt, pools of water, piles of gray bricks and stones, and into a courtyard surrounded by a two-story building with a balcony running all the way around the second story. We climbed up some ladder-steps and were greeted by the woman, her husband, children, and relatives. Flowers in pots were on the balcony railing outside the rooms, along with such necessities as wood, pots and pans, and clothes drying. The inside of her house was as clean as a whistle. Many hours must have been spent cleaning it up. We sat on a low bed, which was at right angles to another with a table in front of us. She sat in a chair facing us. Rugs covered the beds. The floor was bare and spotless. Our hostess was beautiful: red cheeks, black hair, and a lovely expression. She was born a serf; she and her family worked for a man who owned seven or eight slaves. She carried water and looked after horses and cattle. She was fourteen at the time of Liberation. She had no education but said she attended the factory school a bit. However, she can barely read and cannot write. In addition to cleaning up the house, they had borrowed some books, which were prominently displayed on top of one of the painted cupboards: the complete works of Mao, which they said they studied at night, and some novels in Chinese, which they don't understand. Harrison says many people in underdeveloped countries and societies do this to impress visitors with the fact they are literate, which in most cases they are not. Touching, but rather ridiculous, too.

Her husband was also born a serf. Now he is a policeman in the Registration of Population Department,

114

whatever that means. He had been drinking and couldn't stop talking, kept interrupting us and his wife constantly. Tibetans drink a lot of barley beer, and they enjoy drinking.

This couple have three children, the first born at home, the next two in the hospital. There is a clinic in the neighborhood where children get innoculations. Her mother and father live next door and help with the children. We saw their room, and it wasn't as spic and span as where we sat.

All through the visit we were urged to drink yak butter tea, or just butter tea as they called it in Sikkim. It is made of butter (often rancid), flour, sugar, tea, and salt, and it is one of the few things in the world I can't bear to taste. It is always offered to guests, and it is rude not to drink some. But it is well-nigh impossible for me without gagging. Harrison is better at swallowing it than I am, but I wonder if it can be as awful to him as it is to me. Anyway, I made an effort, but they would really like us to drink cup after cup, and a few sips is probably just as rude as not drinking it at all. I hope I didn't hurt her feelings.

We asked about the Dalai Lama and how they felt about him. She said she doesn't want him to come back, doesn't want any return to the past, doesn't believe in any religion, and thinks life is better for everyone now. When she was a child, she went to the temple, but hasn't gone since Liberation. Her parents do go, as do many older people.

Tonight before dinner, we had a meeting with the vice-chairman or vice-governor, of Tibet. He is Tibetan, as is the chairman, or governor. Harrison made another plug for our going to Nepal. He told about our experience in Sikkim when we crawled across a landslide minutes after the Indian Army had dynamited it to remove some huge boulders that had landed in the road. There was an army jeep waiting on the other side, and the Indians drove us to our destination, Bagdogra Airport. He suggested that the Chinese army had helicopters here and said he was sure the Chinese army would be more helpful than the Indian army. I don't think it did any good. I am convinced the Chinese have made up their minds that we are going back to Chengdu. It is frustrating to be so helpless about what we are going to do. The Nepalese Consul General says he is going to drive to Katmandu himself in a few days. I wish we could go with him.

We learned a lot at this meeting, mainly that the Chinese now realize that terrible mistakes have been made here and they seem to be trying to recoup what's left and go forward with ways and means that are Tibetan, not Chinese. The ideal is to have Tibetans run their country, though, of course, under Chinese suzerainty. Work and programs must be planned and carried out by Tibetan leadership working together with Tibetan masses. Such communist language! At present they said, the cadres are 50 percent Han (Chinese) and 50 percent Tibetan. (A cadre is a man or woman who is trained especially in Communist ideology and is sent out to promote the doctrine.) I have been told, not here, that in the first years of the Chinese occupation Tibetans felt like second-class citizens in their own country. They needed an interpreter to communicate with the Chinese. The Chinese looked down on Tibetans, regarded them as inferior, even animals, and did not bother to learn their language. Now some Chinese speak Tibetan, and some Tibetans have been sent to Beijing to learn the dogma and have returned home to help implement it.

It remains incredible to me that the Red Guards were

permitted to do such insane things in the Cultural Revolution. For instance, they labeled ownership capitalistic, limited cattle ownership to three, confiscated the remaining livestock, and slaughtered most of the yak. Tibetans have always depended on animals that can stand the altitude because not many crops can grow this high up. Even though they are Buddhists and don't believe in killing for food, their diet has consisted mainly of meat products. They have gotten around this by having special butchers to do the slaughtering. These men were considered lower than the low. Barley has always been the staple grain. The Chinese plowed up grazing land and planted rice and wheat, which did not flourish. That, plus killing the animals, created a terrible food shortage. Formerly every household produced wool for itself and to sell, to Nepal, Bhutan, Sikkim, Shanghai. This automatically ceased with the slaughter of animals. So the people suffered, though not as much as most of the upper class who did not leave in 1959, when the Dalai Lama escaped to India.

But now, with the end of the Gang's influence and with the sensible programs of Deng Hsaio-ping, perhaps these excesses can be ameliorated and some progress made in making a better life for these poor people who have suffered so much. Communes will have responsibility for their own programs of planting crops and setting their own quotas. Private plots and ownership of animals is encouraged. Everything will be done to try to raise the living standard and welfare.

There was also talk about the Dalai Lama and whether he will return. I think Harrison feels that the Chinese want him back, that perhaps he could unite the country the way they have not been able to do. They realize that many Tibetans still regard him as their leader. He would

117

be more than just the religious figurehead; the Chinese only want to control foreign affairs and the military, they said. The Dalai Lama is surrounded by advisors and ministers, and I wonder what they would do. And I wonder, if he did come back, what would all the people who left with him do? There are many in India, but also in other countries. Would they want to return? Could this new regime incorporate them? So many questions.

After that meeting we were dinner guests of the vice-chairman. We sat behind the screen in the dining room where we eat our meals, separated tonight from our fellow visitors, the Hong Kong photographer, the French tourists, and the American doctor and his wife. At dinners you usually start with a plate for hors d'oeuvres that are already on the table. Then, as new dishes are brought in, you just put portions on the same plate. If there are bones or pieces you can't or don't want to eat, your plate is removed and you get a clean one. Tonight's dinner was enormous, dish after dish kept appearing. Our little local guide sat by me and kept piling mountains of food on my plate so that I ended up with two so full they had to be taken away to make room for more. It is so odd to think anyone can consume so much, especially in this altitude when everyone knows the less you eat, the better off you are. It's sickening, too, to have so much extra when there are people who are probably hungry right outside the door.

Thursday, August 21
Lhasa

LAST NIGHT I stayed awake until after 2:00, then slept until 6:15. I felt seedy this morning, but even now I don't feel a bit sleepy. The American doctor gave me some pills, which I will take as soon as I finish this. I hope they'll work. This is the only real effect the altitude has on me, and though it isn't like being sick, it's tiring.

This morning we set off for what we were told was to be a picnic by the side of the river and an exhibit of horsemanship and native songs and dances. After we'd gone about five minutes, Li announced we were going 40 miles (60 kilometers) away and wouldn't be back until evening. We had understood it was quite close, and since H. wanted to call the Nepalese again, we had to turn around and go back for him to do that.

It certainly wasn't 40 miles; nearer 15, I'd say. The sun and air and stream were wonderful, the show strictly for tourists, and the lunch not exactly appetizing. The Lindblad group was also there; in fact, it was arranged for them and we just went along as extra guests.

A typical Tibetan tent, which is a big square canvas stretched flat between four posts—just a roof, the sides open—was set up by the side of the river. There were a few chairs, low tables, and lots of rugs, so most people sat on the ground. I got a chair and sat out in the sun. First we had the exhibit of horsemanship which really didn't amount to anything. The men and horses were all dressed up in bright-colored clothes, blankets, and harness and looked as if they were going to be in a movie, and they raced back and forth by us. The only trick or skill they exhibited was to pick something up off the ground while galloping—the same thing we saw the Kazaks do in China. Several tourists, among them H. and Li, rode the horses, and one American woman bought the red hat off a Tibetan for the equivalent of $24, more than he sees in a year. I can't believe she would be crazy enough to put it on her head. All the children must have lice, and grown-ups must, too. The children are so filthy I hate to have them come near me, which is awful. Several had the most terrible eruptions on their faces. Some of the girls and women are really beautiful—but oh, the dirt.

Children danced and sang while a large black yak meandered along in the river paying no heed to the music or the tourists, who rushed to take his picture. Yaks are the most remarkable-looking animals, more like our buffalo than anything else, with big wide horns, a bushy tail and long heavy hair that hangs down around them like a skirt. Usually they are black, domesticated yaks are black and white, and I have seen dark brown and gray yaks. They can stand as high as six feet (two meters). Tibetans depend on yaks for almost everything: meat, milk, butter, and wool, which is made into felt or cloth. Musical horns and different objects are made from the yak horns. Boots, pouches, bags, harness, and many necessities from the hide. All the more terrible that so many were slaughtered during the Cultural Revolution.

The Lindblad guides had brought napkins and beer, which they shared with us. Lunch consisted of hard-boiled eggs, bread, mutton, yogurt with sugar, which was quite good, and *tsampa*. This is the staple grain food of Tibetans. They eat it for breakfast and often at other meals. It is made of barley mixed up with butter tea. A Tibetan rolls it into a firm ball; today's was already made into cake forms. The mutton was boiled and served in big

120

hunks with fat and bones. I asked one of the Lindblad group if he had enjoyed his lunch. Not amused, he answered, "And what do you mean by 'enjoy'?"

Anyway, it didn't last all day, though I think Li wished it had. He's having the adventure of his life on this trip, even if he has gotten sick several times. We wanted to leave right after the picnic, so we walked up to our car, which had been parked near the road above the river. The bus that brought the other people was in the way and Li said we couldn't go until they did. We suggested he find the driver and ask him to move the bus. He didn't think that was a good idea, so I went over to the bus and there was the driver sitting in it. I asked him to move so we could get out and that was that. I guess people brought up under this kind of government are so accustomed to accepting whatever is, without questioning, that we seem strangely independent when we suggest that there might be another way or that something might be changed. It would never occur to them to ask for anything different.

When we got back to Lhasa, H. had another talk with Li about our leaving. It now seems to have boiled down to a bureaucratic impasse between the highway people and the locals here. So H. asked Li to try to get Foreign Minister Huang Hua on the phone so that he could talk to him about it. Li was aghast but said he would. Perhaps that will work. The Nepalese still say the road is passable.

Because we got back earlier than expected, we had time to see the Summer Palace, or Norbulingka, in Treasure, or Jewel Park. As we have noticed before, everything has two or three names. We drove a little way out from the town and stopped in front of a white gate with a tiled roof. Two large white lions decorated in several bright colors stood guard at each side of the door.

It looks like the gatehouse to the palace in Sikkim. In fact, everything we see that isn't Chinese reminds me of Sikkim, which is natural because most of Sikkim's culture and religion is Tibetan.

With Harrison at the Summer Palace

We were expected, so the door was opened at the toot of the car's horn. The only building we saw was the palace that was either built or redone by the present Dalai Lama in 1954–56. Everyone says something different, but the park itself was started in the eighteenth century by the seventh Dalai Lama and finished by the thirteenth. But I suppose one can say it was never finished because even now all kinds of digging and construction are going on in the park. They were redoing an old bridge and putting in new drains; the house itself needs plenty of work. Fundamentally it is a pretty, fairly grand Tibetan house that also looks a little like a temple. It is two stories high and has a center part and two wings. The doorways are beautiful, carved wood in bright colors. The rooms are pretty in the mixed-up Tibetan fashion with gorgeous little carved tables, done with inlaid enamel tops. In the Dalai Lama's dressing room there is a big Phillips radio, a record player with an Indian-made Victor record of Buddhist prayers and chanting on it, as if someone had just been playing it. In his bedroom he had a radio, a separate record player, and an electric fan. His bedroom is the smallest room we saw and had a simple iron bed. There are two regular bathrooms, one on each side of the upstairs. In one the toilet seat was broken and askew.

It is a charming house on a human livable scale, set in gardens and a little park of trees. You look out and up to the mountains. The Dalai Lama preferred living here to life in the Potala, and I don't blame him. Though we haven't been inside the Potala yet, I can't believe any part of it is as homey and attractive as this house. The gardens look like English or European flower beds, and I think Heinrich Harrar had a lot to do with planning them. He was the German who was arrested and imprisoned by the British in India when World War II began. He escaped and made his way to Tibet, experiencing many fantastic adventures. When he had been in Lhasa for a while, he became friendly with the young Dalai Lama and spent quite a lot of time with him. He says in his book, *Seven Years in Tibet*, that he laid out the gardens and built the wall around this park.

We walked back to the gate, which was shut and locked, and we waited quite a while until the woman who keeps the keys was found. This is a park for the people, we are told, but I don't see how they get in. It certainly isn't "open to the public."

123

Afterwards Li joined us for a stroll around the back of the Potala, through a rather dirty park with a childrens' playground, seesaws, swings, and a sort of jungle gym. There were two circles of barbed wire about 4 feet (1.2 meters) apart and about 20 feet (7 meters) across, and we wondered what for.

Just before supper Li came to tell us that the road is improving and we should be able to get through with maybe a few days delay. So it won't be necessary to call Huang Hua!! I wonder if the idea of a complaint to the top made some of the petty bureaucrats involved in this whole silly impasse more flexible. Anyway, Harrison is elated and I am relieved.

At 9:00 the Nepalese sent their car for us, and at the consulate they showed us slides. Many were of the road over which we now believe we may be traveling; the rest were of Nepal and Tibet. The consul general has a simple hand-worked projector, and he showed the pictures on the wall. He has some wonderful pictures of mountains and of Mount Everest, which can be seen from the road to Nepal. In the middle of all the slides he showed us a dapper, handsome man sitting under an awning with two other men. "He was my friend," he said. "He died." The next few pictures were of this man being chopped up like a goat and given to the vultures. I know this is customary when a person dies in Tibet. The Tibetans have never buried their dead. In the past important lamas were embalmed and gilded and put in temples as objects of worship. But when an ordinary person dies, he is carried to a flat rock, dismembered, and given to vultures. The skull is crushed and burned with the bones, although there is not enough wood for total cremation.

"Sometimes the vultures don't like the meat," said our host. "It may be diseased and then the pieces are burned."

It was like an outdoor slaughterhouse. In one picture we saw the friend sitting under the awning; in the next we saw a skinned, dead body face down on a huge rock. Two men with big knives squatted next to the body. "Now they are cutting him up," said our host as he changed the slide. Two other bodies were added. Buzzards sat in rows, waiting patiently as if they were trained. The two other bodies still had the skin on when we first saw them, but in progressive slides we saw them being cut up and arranged just as in a butcher shop. The entrails and insides were on one side, the bones and meat on another. The birds wait until told to eat. The skulls are crushed with heavy blows, and after everything is picked clean, the remains are burned in a sort of wood-lattice round thing that looks like the roll-up baby pen we put the youngest grandchildren in outdoors when they come to visit. The consul general didn't say what is done with the ashes, if anything. The slides were all in color.

Now for the sleeping pills!

Friday, August 22
Lhasa

THE PILLS WORKED. I went to sleep at 11:00 and Harrison woke me at 7:45. Wow!! What a difference sleep makes!

The Nepalese told us last night that the Chinese had called them to ask what *they* knew about the road. They told the Chinese that they knew the Nepalese side had been repaired, mail and buses have already come through to Lhasa. We think now that the Chinese are afraid of losing face if they have to admit they haven't fixed their side. The latest we have been told is that probably we can go that route, though we may have to walk several kilometers. So we wired—or, rather, the Nepalese wired for us—Ambassador Trimble that we are hoping to arrive on August 28, less than a week away. I can hardly believe it. There have been several times on this trip when I thought I couldn't stand it anymore. I have always heard that Asia, the Orient, gets Westerners down after a while. But it's supposed to be a matter of years, not weeks. Occasionally I have felt that I couldn't for even one more hour stand the dust, the dirt, the noise, the constant jabbering. The hawking and spitting—out the car window, all over the streets, into spitoons—is unpleasant; and here in Lhasa you have to be on constant alert not to step in human excreta.

This morning we went to the Jokhang Temple in the heart of old Lhasa. It is the oldest temple in Lhasa and for centuries was, and still is, the seat of Tibetan Buddhism, the Buddhist Mecca. Pilgrims have come from all over the world to worship here. Even today people were prostrating themselves on the filthy streets, up the shallow steps, and into the dark entrance hall. Being in the middle of town surrounded by other buildings, it is impossible to imagine its size from the outside. And in my wildest dreams I couldn't have pictured what we saw inside at every turn. Harrison wrote that it was "a conglomerate of filth and superstitions—a journey into the Dark Ages—a descent into medieval Hell." Like Europe in the thirteenth century.

All around the first hall are little shrines, each one crammed with Buddhas, statues, butter lamps, water bowls. Also crammed with believers fingering and kissing the fabric on the statues, fabric stiff with the black grease and grime of thousands of dirty fingers and lips. Making offerings of whatever they have—money, string, thread, buttons, and many safety pins pinned to the dirty raveling cloth. Bowing and bowing to the statues, mumbling and chanting prayers, asking to be made well, for help, for care. The crowd moved slowly swaying from side to side from shrine to shrine, and hundreds more people waited in the middle of the hall for their turn. The special shrine for the sick was so jammed no one could get in. The smell was unbelievable from unwashed clothes and bodies and the special sour, oily smell of the butter lamps. Some of the monks wore nose masks as they made the rounds refilling lamps. I think there must be every known germ in there.

The propaganda is that only old people go to the temple, but everyone was here. Young mothers with babies on their backs; children; teen-age boys and girls, young men who—even in the temple, and in spite of our Chinese escorts—pulled silver objects from inside their coats, offering them for sale. The monks said that about 3,000 people come every day to worship and nearer six thousand on holidays.

We climbed the steps to the upper balconies, and here we found a different world. The floors are swept and clean, everything is open, the balconies rising higher than anything else in the town. The doors have wonderful bronze handles. Carved gilded birds, animals, bells, decorations abound in the heavenly clear air. On the highest roof are the two gilded deer that adorn most Tibetan temples, gazing at the wheel of life, or law. They are symbolic of Buddha talking in the Deer Park, setting in motion the wheel of law.

The flat rooftops of the buildings, that look so dirty

from the street, are nice, and children were playing on them and flying kites. Much better than playing down below in the manure and mud and filth. There is a great view of the Potala Palace, the city, and the valley.

It is not clear if monks live here, or how many, if any. A visitor who speaks Tibetan told me that one monk said, "Don't be fooled by seeing so many of us here." He said they only spent a short time in the temple; most of the time they worked in the fields.

This temple was ravaged during the Cultural Revolution, we were told. Local Tibetans took part along with the Chinese Red Guards, and there was a lot of looting besides wanton destruction. Many of the good objects offered for sale in the market came from here, evidently. Some parts of the temple are being repaired and restored, but it is a huge job. Artists and workers have to be trained, and most frescos and paintings have to be done practically from scratch.

The guides know very little about Tibet, Buddhism, the buildings, or what anything means. I believe the Chinese are teaching and training people in Beijing and are spending money restoring some temples and monasteries, but more as tourist attractions than places of worship.

On the way home we went to see a mosque, on the same grimy alley-street we walked down to visit the woman who worked in the rug factory. The mosque is a mess, small and full of junk. Just outside the gate was a meat counter with a woman selling joints and cuts of mutton and goat.

Our guest house is at right angles to another guest house, and the Dalai Lama's sister is staying there. When we got back from the temple, there was a huge crowd, about 800 people, waiting to catch a glimpse of her.

Several members of his family have been here recently; a certain amount of politiking must be going on. I wonder what she thinks of what's happened here and how the country looks. We have been told that there are only about 10 monasteries left out of nearly 2,500, and the number of monks has been reduced from 120,000 to 2,000.

After lunch and our usual rest, we set out for a tour of the Potala Palace. We went to its base at the bottom of the hill. It is possible to drive about halfway up in a jeep along a stone path wide enough for a car. The path winds up from the back of the palace until it meets the stone steps that go the rest of the way. The Potala feels like a medieval city built on the top of a hill, with steps and alleys almost perpendicular. We met doors and gates at every turn and windows looked down on us from dizzying heights. Our car could only go a short way, so

Potala Palace in Tibet

we walked the rest. It was terribly steep, but I went slowly, so didn't get too out of breath. There was an oxygen bag in the car in case we needed it, but by the time we got to the top the oxygen was a long way off.

The Potala that we see today was planned and started by the fifth Dalai Lama in the seventeenth century on the foundation of Songtsen Gampo's palace. The Dalai Lama died before it was finished, and the regents (who rule when a Dalai Lama is a child, or incapacitated) first announced that the Dalai Lama was ill, then that he had gone into meditation. For ten years this story was kept up until the Potala was completed.

In spite of the setting and grandeur, the riches, the statues of gold and silver imbedded with jewels, the brocades, the carved and inlaid furniture, the Potala is the spookiest place I have ever been. The rooms where the Dalai Lama lived are at the top, a series of small rooms stuffed with furniture, curtains, hangings, murals, objects. Overdecorated, overcarpeted, overhung. Everything overdone except comfort. At least there was light from the windows. Since the Potala is so huge, only the outside rooms have light. The palace descends from the rooms at the top, through hundreds, maybe thousands more, down to the storerooms where treasures were kept, and on down to the dungeons. Some of the halls have light from above, since there are balconies and open spaces occasionally, the way there are in the Jokhang Temple.

Besides being the living quarters of the Dalai Lama and the seat of government and power, it is also the burial place of most of the Dalai Lamas. Their bodies were embalmed sitting in the lotus position, then encased in silver or gold or both. A tower or spire rose from that, encrusted with jewels and precious stones. One of these stupas, or *chortens*, is 70 feet (20 meters) high, the gold spires rising up above the roof.

The richness of Asian monuments amazes me, and here in this dark and sinister palace, in the midst of poverty and ignorance and dirt, I am stunned once more. The Red Guards did terrible damage to the Potala, and enormous restoration is going on. In nearly every hall or temple carpenters and painters are at work. Quite a few Tibetans followed us as we made our tour, and again people were prostrating themselves in front of the altars.

Harrison says the Potala is "dreadful, dark, evil, superstitious." It is all of those and more. But it is probably the most fantastic, bizarre and terrifying place I have ever seen. It would be awful to live in it. No wonder the Dalai Lama preferred the Summer Palace.

This evening after supper we met with two Tibetans who have somehow managed to survive since 1959. One was a woman in her forties, I'll call her Mary. She is beautiful, strong, calm, and controlled. She speaks English, so we could talk together. Our English-speaking escorts and guides were present, but nevertheless everyone was very frank. I was amazed. Her story is typical of what happened to upper- or noble-class families who did not escape with the Dalai Lama when he fled to India. Her husband was imprisoned by the Chinese and remained in jail for sixteen years. He is out now, freed last year, and is a member of an important government council. It is clear from what we heard tonight that the Chinese realize they must have qualified Tibetans help them to put this country in some sort of order. Most of the educated Tibetans who didn't leave in 1959 or later were put in jail by the Chinese and only recently released. Schools have been established, and Tibetan people who were slaves before 1959 can now be

131

educated. But there hasn't been time to build up a new generation that is capable of governing their country. The upper-class Tibetans are needed.

Mary has three children. The two older are uneducated because she "could not afford to send them to school." Harrison feels the Chinese didn't let them go to school, and then, of course, for ten years the schools were closed during the Cultural Revolution. These two have simple manual jobs, but the youngest is at school now.

She told us she could never live through anything like that period again. It was "very hard." "How shall I say?" she kept repeating. She was made to apologize to the people for the fact of her birth into an upper-class family. Under the Gang she did physical labor. "You lived off the backs of the people," the crowds shouted at her. Day after day she was made to bow down in front of large gatherings to apologize and confess that she had lived off the backs of the people. This went on all over China in those dark days. Teachers, professors, writers, poets, artists, people who were born into well-to-do families, people who differed ideologically, were made to kneel on a platform in front of mass meetings, were forced to confess their "crimes," were subjected to humiliation and hate, were stoned by youngsters who were paid a penny apiece to throw stones at their elders. Sometimes they were killed.

Many of the noble- and upper-class families of Tibet have intimate ties with Sikkim. The chogyal, or king, of that little country, which has been incorporated into India, is himself Tibetan, and his first wife was also. His second wife, as most Americans know, was Hope Cooke from New York. In the past there was close contact between the two countries, flourishing trade as well as visiting back and forth among families and friends.

Mary kept saying, "Life is much better now." They can see foreigners (I wondered how many.) A relative, a princess of Sikkim, came to visit via Nepal. She told Mary that the chogyal had married an American, the first she had heard of it. The wedding was in 1963. Her parents and a sister are in India, she did not hear from them in all those years since 1959. But now she was hoping to be allowed to visit them. The parents wanted to see her once more "before they leave this earth." (We were told later in the United States that she, her husband, and two children were visiting in India. One child had to remain in Lhasa.)

Over and over she repeated how much better life is now. I couldn't bring myself to ask her for any details about herself. She has suffered deeply; it is written all over her face.

A Tiebetan man, tall and handsome, also a member of one of the former prominent families, told us he had worked as a laborer during the years after 1959. He has the biggest hands I ever saw. He has six children—"all laborers," he said. He started to tell us that his children were uneducated, but the translator interrupted with, "They all speak Chinese as well as their own language." However, that doesn't mean they went to school or were able to study.

Both these Tibetan people think the Dalai Lama should come back. The Tibetans are a religious people, and they need him, they said.

It was a devastating experience for us, and when we said good-bye I burst into tears. It was as if one of my own children had suffered like that.

133

Saturday, August 23
Lhasa

IN THE MORNING we drove back on the road to the airport for about five or six miles (eight or nine kilometers) to the Zhe Bang, or Drepung, Monastery. It is the biggest monastery here now and covers the mountainside. It is like an old town in almost any very old country in Europe, Asia, or Africa. Though the living quarters for the monks may be dark and terrible inside, outside it consists of tiny streets and steps winding up hills and around corners with two and three stories attached, white stucco buildings with blue-painted windows. Flowers grow helter-skelter, and here and there were tiny vegetable gardens.

At the Drepung Monastery

We climbed from terrace to terrace, and from each level went up steep steps to fine halls and shrines with hundreds of statues, bowls, and lamps. Potted plants were clustered by a door, the temples and shrines are open, compared with others we have seen—lighter, airier, less smelly. There is a feeling of outdoors, and the view over the valley is breathtaking. This is what Tibet means to me, or rather what I used to imagine it was. Snowcapped mountains, brilliant blue sky, thick white clouds, clean clear air, monasteries on all the hills and mountains.

The Drepung Monastery was built in the fifteenth century. The early Dalai Lamas are entombed here in funeral pagodas and there is a famous library of Tibetan works. In some of the halls the columns are wrapped around with heavy brocade. This, too, suffered damage during the Cultural Revolution and is being repaired. Up until 1959, 7,700 monks lived here. Today there are 248. They "engage in agriculture" when they are not tending the water bowls and butter lamps.

Most of the monks I've seen are old, filthy, almost toothless, wrapped around in dark red robes that I'm sure have never been washed. They sit polishing the silver bowls, sweeping up offerings of grain, or tending the water and candles. There are many humble offerings, as in the Jokhang Temple; the drapery on the statues almost completely covered with safety or straight pins, all a person had to give.

It is a heavenly place in spite of the shabbiness that is everywhere. We bought some apples from the monks before we left.

In the afternoon four Tibetan leaders came to see H. One was a big lama who lives at the Drepung Monastery. He is sixty-seven years old but seemed a thousand. Very big, very bulky in his orange robe. He wore prayer beads on his left wrist. He used a cane and had to be helped up from his chair and down the stairs. He seemed twitchy and removed, took a few snorts of snuff or something. H. asked him what role Buddhism could play in the reconstruction of Tibet, and he replied he didn't see any possible role. He said the Dalai Lama could come back and be very helpful, but he would have to recognize and stay within the present government policy; that Tibet is part of China and will never be independent. If he cannot go along with that policy, he would do no good for Tibet. Most of the time this old lama slept, and the man sitting next to him would nudge him awake occasionally. When they left, he was very genial.

The second man wore a felt hat and looked like a cowboy. He is fifty and used to be a magistrate of Dingri County. Magistrates had a lot of power because there wasn't any real law in Tibet. I have no idea what happened to him during the bad years; we didn't ask him. He is now vice-chairman of the Chinese People's Consultative Conference of Tibet. He thinks the Dalai Lama should come back and that he can make a great contribution within the Communist Party. It is useless for him to stay outside. People who left Tibet in 1959, or at any time, are now welcome back, he said, though they weren't for many years.

The third man was a tiny, hunched-over man with shaved head. He is fifty-seven years old and also a member of an important committee. He is a Living Buddha of the Remachi Monastery.

The fourth man is only thirty-two. He is another Living Buddha. There are eight Living Buddhas, incarnations, who rule in rotation if the Dalai Lama is young or ill. (Not under present circumstances, obviously.) It is interesting that they are still called this now. How does it all mesh with Communist Party dogma? How do they really view themselves? This man, also, is on a government committee.

All four would welcome the Dalai Lama back. The only person we talked to who wouldn't is the woman factory worker. But, they said, Tibet has changed, the Dalai Lama must have a good picture of what it is like now, not as he remembers or imagines it. The fact that members of his family and others have come here in the past two years may mean that he has had some change of mind. They seem to think it shows a willingness on his part to return.

H. asked about the Tibetan marriage customs, which have always been so bizarre. To keep property in the family, fathers and sons could marry the same woman if the son's mother were dead. Often three brothers shared the same wife. In 1960 the marriage law was passed making polygamy and polyandry illegal. These men feel the new law is pretty much observed except out in remote villages.

I wondered if the old lama's feebleness and the crooked back of the third man were the results of harsh treatment.

This is our last night in Lhasa. We leave tomorrow for Shigatse—first stop on the road to Nepal. I never thought it would work out this way and am full of admiration for Harrison's determination and perseverance. He told me how much this Tibet trip is costing, and I am staggered. Almost $2,000 for Tibet alone. Everything is terribly expensive here. We heard the Lindblad tours, which start in Hong Kong, cost $4,500 or more. And they are here seven days.

I haven't mentioned that there are many dogs here in Lhasa, a violent contrast with China, where we never see them and only in Dunhuang did I hear them. Here they are all over the place, sleeping all day in the streets and alleys. We are told that Tibetans love dogs and every family has at least one for a pet. The only breed I recognize is the Lhasa Apsa. They bark at night, so maybe they're for protection, too. From what I have observed, Tibetans are rough with animals, jerking and hitting horses and donkeys and kicking dogs.

Sunday, August 24
Shigatse

WE LEFT LHASA in slightly threatening weather, the clouds low over the city. We had our last look at the Potala, that dark and sinister place. H. says he feels a little better about it, having seen the Dalai Lama's rooms at the top. But the thought of what used to go on in the lower rooms and prisons is overpowering and cancels out most other impressions. A strange, sad city; a gorgeous, terrifying palace; poor raggedy people, a sixteenth-century culture, and the Chinese Communist army all mixed up in this naturally beautiful country.

We are traveling in a minibus, which is not the ideal vehicle for these roads. I believe Lhasa has eight Land Rovers, and six are out in the country and the Dalai Lama's sister has one, maybe two. The French journalist we met has one. Also I guess they weren't counting on us making this trip; they didn't know how persistent H. can be. But we have lots of room, and if we don't break down or get stuck it will be fine. We are just us, Li, and two Chinese drivers who are also mechanics. One drives much too fast, and we are afraid he'll wreck the car. The road doesn't worry us half as much as this. The second driver is very cautious, but he only drove for a short while today.

We drove to the junction of the Lhasa and Brahmaputra rivers, where the road to the airport goes east. We went west. So many rivers start in Tibet. The Yangtze, Yellow, Mekong, and Salween. The Irrawaddy, Indus, and the Brahmaputra, called the Tsangpo in Tibet. It flows for 800 miles (1,300 kilometers) through Tibet before reaching India.

We drove all day through mountains on roads like those in Sikkim, up to as high as 14,000 feet (4,000 meters) and more. At times snow-covered peaks were very near on either side. Rushing, clear streams, which turned brown and smooth as we got down into the valley. No traffic, but on one turn H. looked back and saw an army truck going round the curves we had come over. He was relieved: help in case we broke down or got stuck. We did get stuck momentarily in a wet spot where water came pouring down from the mountains onto the road, but we got out quickly. I said we should have a shovel, and perhaps we can find one here.

On the mountain slopes great herds of sheep, goats, and yak. No trees at this height, but green grass and brush. Farther down were the most beautiful colors of fields of red barley, yellow rape, red millet, blue lupins. Many other mountain flowers. We stopped several times to see how much they are like ours. We passed many ruins of houses and temples. The Chinese say all destruction was due to the Red Guards and the Cultural Revolution. Though they did go completely wild in Tibet, I don't

139

believe that entirely. The Chinese sacked a lot at various times, so did the Tibetans, not to mention Mongols and other invaders. Nestled back in the crevices of mountains and at the beginning of the wonderful valley are remnants of what must have been noble family houses and monasteries. Some are complete wrecks, half covered with sand and dirt and abandoned. Some have Tibetans living in them. The villages are colorless and barren. The flat-top, one-story houses are labyrinths of stone. In a tiny settlement outside a house like this a group of girls was sitting on the ground in front of a big blackboard. A man was writing on it. A school of sorts, maybe adult education, teaching illiterate Tibetans how to read.

About an hour from here we saw a fairly well preserved town with a temple, slightly reminiscent of Italy and the hill towns. There had been a wall all around the city and the city offices were in a fort on the hill. But that's all gone now. Only a bit of the wall remains. The Red Guards finished off what the townspeople hadn't taken care of. It's like looking at a skeleton.

Near and in the villages many people, men and women, pushing, pulling, and carrying huge loads: stones, bags of stuff, junk mostly.

Our quarters here in Shigatse are in one of those guest houses built like a motel without bathrooms. Our room is okay, beds comfortable, nice comforter, thick rugs on the floor. We go through a huge sitting room, a meeting room actually, to get to our room. It has several sofas and many armchairs. Looking down on the grandeur are big pictures of Mao and Hua. A woman comes into our room every few minutes with hot water. She pours what is left in the Thermos jugs into a kettle for us to wash and refills the Thermos bottles.

The WC is the usual kind with no water, terribly

140

smelly but fairly clean. I have the most difficult time because I have to hold a handkerchief to my nose the whole time I'm in there or it is unbearable, and to manage everything else with one hand is not easy. We wash in the tin basins, brush our teeth with water from a cup, and spit into the spitoon.

There is a large contingent of Chinese in Tibet waiting to go back to Beijing. They have been here ten to twenty years. As we have been told so often, the new policy is to have Tibetans manage their own affairs. The Chinese have trained Tibetan cadres, but I can't imagine how they can manage by themselves. They haven't had enough time to develop a "socialistic" point of view. They are still a very feudal society, and when a person gets a little authority, he lords it over those under him. Of course, that happens in communist societies. I have seen elevator men and head waitresses in the Soviet Union be dreadful to people who depend on them, just to show their power. The Tibetans are so ignorant, so backward; it must be terribly difficult for Chinese to have to live out here so long. I don't see why they aren't rotated every two or three years. But I suppose that would be expensive.

They are happy about leaving, and there is a pleasant, almost holiday atmosphere in the guest house. The Chinese brush their teeth as we do, using a cup of water. But most of them do it outdoors and spit any old place. Tonight when we came back from dinner, a man was sitting on the little terrace outside our room brushing his teeth vigorously and spitting just over the wall.

We ate dinner at one end of a huge room that is being used as a carpentry shop. Tables and benches are stacked all over, saw horses and shavings and sawdust. Our chauffeurs and Li sat at one table, we sat at another. A group of French geologists sat across the room. They have

141

been here about fifteen days, seven men and one woman. They are working with and advising the Chinese about what minerals may be in the mountains. At dinner they wanted some wine; they had used up what they had brought. The waiter couldn't understand, so they asked Li to help. He explained there is no wine here. The French were flabbergasted—they couldn't believe it— and had to settle for beer.

Monday, August 25
Shigatse

WE HAVE A nice, genial little host, who this morning took us to the Za shen lun bu Monastery. According to the archives in the monastery, it was founded in 1447 by the brother of the first Dalai Lama. When he died, the construction was continued by the fourth, fifth, and sixth Panchen Lamas. (It is hard to explain in a simple way the complicated relationship of the Dalai and Panchen Lamas. Best to say, the first Panchen Lama was the teacher of the great fifth Dalai Lama. In gratitude, the Dalai Lama declared that his teacher was an incarnation and bestowed on him this monastery in Shigatse, for his headquarters, so to speak, the way the Dalai Lama had the Drepung, Sera, and Ganden Monasteries at Lhasa. There has been political and religious rivalry between them for years, the Panchen Lamas, on the whole, being pro-Chinese. The present Panchen Lama seems to have followed along that line. He has been in Beijing for many years.

It is a mass of buildings clustered on the mountainside and was, and is, one of the great monasteries of Tibet. It seemed to us to be filled with an enormous amount of gold, silver, and jewels, and the most wonderful copper vessels for butter, wax, holy water, and so on. There is a huge statue of a Buddha, 85 feet (26 meters) high—the biggest copper statue of Buddha in the world, we were told.

We climbed up to the top, and it was wonderful, as always, on the roofs, so near to those great gold animals, birds, dragons, and other figures. And heavenly to look out over the whole valley. This monastery was badly damaged during the Cultural Revolution. Restoration began in 1972. When I asked how the big Buddha escaped the Red Guards, the answer was that the Administration Office told the Lamas to lock the doors. Why didn't they before? And locked doors didn't usually keep the Red Guards out of any place they wanted to get in. There are 191 lamas here now, and it is open for worship.

The damnedest thing is that a water tank is being erected in the first courtyard as you go in. Great scaffolding and mess. We were appalled, so was Li, and said so. Our escorts said they had "never thought of it." Certainly there should be an overall director of all the restoration and preservation. There seems to be no sensible long-range plan. If the Chinese want tourists and tourist money, they must preserve these historic sites. It was like the irrigation project begun at Crescent Springs, but we were told that had been stopped and would be removed.

Then to the Zong Shan, which used to be the seat of government. It was a "lofty fortress" visible from far away, forming an architectural whole. It was built under

Remains of a former fortress destroyed in the Cultural Revolution, on the way to Shigatse

the Ming Dynasty (1368–1643), enlarged and restored under the Qing (1644–1911). It had halls of sutras (collections of Buddhist doctrines and aphorisms), Buddhas, treasure chambers, and a set of sitting lamas, real and lifelike. This was all destroyed by the Red Guards, and there is nothing but the outline of the wall here and there going up and down and around the hill. Tragedy.

From there we went to the Panchen Lama's residence, built in 1956, same era as the Summer Palace in Lhasa. The gate was locked and we had a hard time finding anyone to let us in. People were living in a long building to the right of the gate, and eventually one of them went around the back of the residence and found the caretaker, who grumpily allowed us to enter. He wouldn't allow H. to take any pictures inside, but I got a few outdoors.

This, too, is a sad sight. Very badly damaged during the Cultural Revolution, and though restoration has

144

begun, it is still a shambles. It is really a nice big house, all the stairs are copper, three flights of double stairs. They would be handsome if they were cleaned. The two-story ceiling in the entrance hall was not damaged, though many paintings were rubbed off the walls. But on the third floor, where there is a ballroom with a gorgeous multicolored marble floor, the exquisitely designed and painted ceiling had been viciously attacked and most of it torn out, exposing the lathes. Besides the destruction of this lovely house, it was robbed and looted. Many doors were shut, so we just saw the middle part and two small rooms upstairs.

The present Panchen Lama left here in 1964 and has not come back. He is now chairman of the Chinese People's Consultative Council and it is up to him if he wants to come back, they said. He was imprisoned by the Chinese for ten years and is now living in Beijing. He saw the Dalai Lama's sister when she was in Beijing, and we understand that they got along very well. We have been told that the Panchen Lama is on good terms with the Dalai Lama, that he is not playing along with the Chinese; neither has he fallen into their hands and become a tool for them. Though he has not been back in Shigatse, he was allowed to go to eastern Tibet where he came from. He did not go to Lhasa.

I also have been told that some Tibetans consider him to be a virtual prisoner of the Chinese, and some Tibetans fear the same fate would befall the Dalai Lama if he were to return.

The Chinese army is everywhere we look here. H. says it is a very important military base. Along the way here he said there were many installations that he feels are not necessarily for outside invaders but for internal trouble and uprisings. We hear that 60 percent of the Chinese cadres will be gone by the end of the year, but that has nothing to do with the army.

Down the valley on the road we came on we visited a monastery that was badly damaged and has not been restored at all. But parts of it still stand and quite a few people live there. It is off the road and back near the hills with old terraced fields around. Seeing it makes me feel I am right about there being old temples and monasteries all along this valley that were once populated and prosperous.

Structurally this is a beauty, small with a two-story cloister. All the paint is worn off, which makes it rather nice and plain, not garish the way so much is. But it looks as if it might fall down any minute. It is like a small village. Many families live here, squatting in corners, making fires too near the walls, pigs wallowing in the pretty courtyard, goats, filthy children. Only one or two monks. They say they will restore it. I hope so. At least keep it from collapsing.

Tonight after supper we took a stroll on the street outside the gate. Every guest house we have visited has been in a compound surrounded by a wall and a gate that is closed at different times. Everyone was out walking, more Chinese than Tibetans. We met a Tibetan who lives in Germany. As we passed we looked at him, and he looked at us. We went by, turned around at the same time, and walked back to each other. He looks Tibetan but he also looks very different from most of the Tibetans we have seen or met. First of all, he wore a blue jogging suit. He was terribly friendly. He has lived in Germany for many years. He came up from Katmandu yesterday, which relieved H., since it proves the road is open all the way. He hasn't been in Tibet since all the big changes. He is going to see his sisters and other family, then going to Beijing.

146

Tuesday, August 26
Dingri

THIS PLACE MAKES Shigatse seem like the Mandarin or the Ritz. The same formation of buildings, rooms with hard mud floors, a door and a window, no screen, no water, an outdoor WC miles away right by the front gate. Very conspicuous.

We left Shigatse about 9:00 (7:00 by the sun), saying good-bye to the beautiful monastery roofs all sparkling gold in the early light. We drove by the Panchen Lama's sad house and on into the seemingly endless fertile plateau-valley. All along the sides of the road were wrecks of buildings, whether from the Cultural Revolution or from uprisings, fighting or just natural causes—no one seems to know. Many were in the midst of bright green terraced farming, a big contrast to the multitude of dry, sandy landscapes we have been through. Most of the buildings were too far away to see, but we could tell that some had once been big establishments and some were remains of temples. Lots of old walls. Sharp, jagged, reddish mountains rimmed the valley. It would seem that every mineral in the world is inside them, but the French geologists said they hadn't found much, at least so far.

At the end of the valley we began to climb up, up, up, higher and higher, to rocky upland, steep pastures. Only scrubby green mosslike stuff grows and we saw no animals or people until we came around a curve. We looked up even farther, and there was a herd of yaks. Incredible. So beautiful, so fantastic that we are in this country and could see such a sight.

Li was sleeping and I began to get a little drowsy when

147

H. shook us both and said, "Wake up, wake up!! We are going over this pass that is seventeen thousand feet high." Really on top of the roof of the world. Harrison said he felt breathless from being tossed around in the car, but I didn't feel any different. However, if we had gotten out and moved, I'm sure I would have.

The road was good except for a few places where the mountain streams wash down. We got stuck in several of these, but Li had got a shovel from a soldier and it helped. The car died twice for no reason that I could understand, but thank goodness for the mechanical know-how of our drivers. They fixed whatever it was each time with not too much delay.

When we first arrived, around 2:00, and were settling into our room, two little boys, probably seven or eight, came and stood in our doorway. Pathetic waifs, dirty, undoubtedly hungry. They hung around, gesticulating, pointing at us, then at themselves. We didn't have anything to give them, and if we had, H. said probably the whole town would be at our door. A Chinese soldier walking by chased them over the wall.

There were lots of beggars in Lhasa and we have heard stories about upper-class family children who, as beggars, were the only source of income for their families after the Liberation.

It is higher here than in Lhasa, and I feel the altitude a bit. But Bufferin seems to take care of my problem, plus the sleeping pills the doctor gave me. I have taken one each night since the first night in Lhasa, when I took two. And I have had no trouble sleeping at all. But Li is sick again and the drivers have taken him to the hospital. There is a Chinese doctor in all these outpost places, fortunately, and they certainly must know how to deal with altitude and travel sickness. I gave Li our oxygen bag,

148

since the other one leaked when a suitcase fell on it in the car. None of us noticed it at the time.

There is nothing to see or do here except observe the people. H. wrote in his notes, "We drove to the heart of the town. It has no heart. Mud houses and streets. Poverty and the ruined fort and wall high above. A fine rushing stream beside it."

Tomorrow we drive to Zhang Mu, about 300 kilometers away, on the Nepalese border. We spend the night there. We have had a message that we will be met. Certainly the Nepalese consul general in Lhasa has been a true friend in need.

Wednesday, August 27
Zhang Mu
On the Nepalese border

WE LEFT DINGRI at nine this morning. Poor Li was barely navigable. We think he suffers from the Chinese fixation about the altitude in Tibet. They *know* they are going to be sick, and they are. Also, Li eats a lot, and I think he'd be better off if he stuck to my diet of soup and tea with only tiny morsels of anything else.

This trip has been a huge responsibility for him. He is only thirty-five; we are older than his parents, and he has been in the role of looking after us. This has been a great adventure for him, going to places he never dreamed he'd go. But it hasn't been easy, especially in Lhasa, when there was so much haggling about our taking this route. I will miss his cheery face and smile. We have been with him for six weeks now, a long time to live so closely with anyone. He has never disappointed us in any way, even when he may have thought we were crazy Americans wanting the impossible.

We hadn't gone far this morning when we encountered a barrier chain across the road with red and white guard posts and two policemen. Our passports and travel documents were inspected and we went through. Very brief and polite. It seems like a funny place to have a checkpoint, so far from the Nepalese border.

The drive was fascinating, starting off on a plateau-valley just like yesterday. Very fertile in spots, and the ruins of a one-time flourishing civilization. Remains of large establishments are quite close together, a series of villages, and what may have been monasteries. Again, I can't believe the Cultural Revolution is responsible for all this. It seems more like the old cities in Xinjiang.

Today we saw thousands of sheep, very small and most had some black on them. Many goats and lots of yaks, gray, brown, and black. They were grazing up on the pastures; down in the valleys they were pack animals, heavily laden with whatever it is that people and animals are always carrying around in Tibet. It is impossible to make out. Off to the south is Mount Everest. I was sure I saw its snowclad peak. H. wasn't so sure. It looked the same as the picture the Nepalese consul general showed us—exactly the same shape.

After the tiny village of Nielamu we drove down the mountain in a valley of waterfalls splashing down thousands of feet. They seem to start in the clouds and fall straight down. Soon we descended to trees and green. It seemed almost tropical after our long stay above the tree line.

There were many signs of road repair, and many places known to be rock falls. The drivers have been over this road before, and each time we came to one of the rock fall places, they would go as fast as possible to avoid any rocks that might be falling. On the side of a straight-up-and-down mountain this was terrifying. One strange thing we had to stop for was logs being pushed from above down to the road. How they are cut down we can't imagine, but they fall in the road in large splintered pieces and are used for firewood, I think. Amazing to see so many trees again.

And here we are, once more at the end of a long trip. We are in a guest house perched on the side of a mountain, down 125 steps from the road. Li counted them. We have a room with a huge bed with a board mattress. Also a sitting room for "resting." We can see and hear the mountain stream rushing by in the valley below us. Such a mammoth change. There are so many flowers, so much green, so many trees, so much mist, so many birds singing (the rarest of all)—it is like a different world.

We arrived here at Zhang Mu, still in China, about 2:30 and spent the afternoon seeing the sights, which are limited, naturally. It is clear that the Chinese are hoping to have tourists here. A hotel is under construction, as is a hospital, and a customs house. We visited the shops where fabric, wool for knitting, a little Chinese wine and beer, soap, towels, and a few other very fundamental items were for sale. We went to the bank, a shack on the hillside, where H. changed our Chinese money into Nepalese, and some back to American. How amazing that they have any U.S. currency here. We saw a monument to the one hundred workers who died while building the road we have just been over. It was opened in 1964, and Harrison is the first American correspondent

151

to travel on it. First of any correspondents, he says. A group from the Smithsonian came this way some time ago, but no journalists. Harrison likes to be the first in places like this.

In 1964 to die building a road was considered like a death in battle. Death in construction. But since the oil rig scandal we talked about at the newspaper in Beijing, this theory has been repudiated.

We have had a delicious dinner; we also had lunch here. The cook is Sichuan. One dish of meatballs and pieces of potato was wonderfully good, along with the rice and soup. Only occasionally on this trip have I not liked the soup. When it was made from fish or was that awfully thick kind that looks like vomit. But usually it is broth with a few thin pieces of vegetables or meat.

We met another Tibetan who is staying here and had a talk after dinner. He lives in the United States, is married to an American. He left Tibet in 1959. He has family in Lhasa and had no contact until recently and doesn't know who is alive or dead. He is traveling on the public bus.

So people are finally being allowed to go back and see their families, after all these years.

Thursday, August 28
Nepal at last—at the ambassador's residence in Katmandu 6:00 P.M., Nepal time

LAST NIGHT, soon after we went to sleep, the most wild thunder and lightning storm woke us up. The skies opened and I have never heard such a downpour. All we could think of was that we would not be able to go even the few miles from Zhang Mu to the Nepalese border. The storm seemed to go all night, but some of the time I believe we mistook the river for rain. H. looked out the window down the valley once and it was clear and bright. But soon after mist rolled in. He hardly slept at all, worrying about the road.

But everything went smoothly. We had hot milk for breakfast and piled into our minibus with two porters who had been hired to carry our stuff over the landslide. Down the narrow road, across two washouts that had been made passable, and to the spot from where the car could go no farther. Harrison was surprised no one was working on the washout. Said it could have been fixed up in half a day. Rather than walking on the road we took the almost straight-down shortcut of about a mile. I'm glad we didn't have to walk up it, which is what our Tibetan friend did yesterday.

At the bottom, in a clearing stood a shabby little pagoda with a stone elephant in front. Down below that the Friendship Bridge, spanning the river. Soldiers on each side, a small settlement on the other. No sign of a car. Once again our hearts sank. Harrison agitated; Li was nervous; I took out my knitting.

We waited well over an hour for the Embassy car to arrive. Just a mix-up because of time difference.

The trip from the Friendship Bridge to Katmandu took nearly four hours and was fascinating every minute of the way. Wherever we were, whatever the scenery, there were millions of children. It was so like Sikkim in many ways, except that the valleys are wider and much of the earth is bright, deep, rusty red. Terracing every possible inch, even high up into the mist which comes and goes, first hiding the narrow fields, then floating away to reveal emerald crops. Lots of spectacular waterfalls at first, until we got out more into the valley. Most Nepalese houses are several stories, usually built into the hillside. Animals live in the bottom floor.

So here we are, in our Embassy, a little piece of the U.S. up here in the Himalayas. I have already had two baths. We will stay here five or six days, long enough for H. to find out what he can about Tibet from this side. Then home.

Epilogue

WE HAVE BEEN home several months now, my diary is typed and at the publishers. Since leaving Tibet we have met and talked with many Tibetan people. Some live in this country, some in Europe, many in India. The trip has settled into me; I have had time to think and reflect on what we saw, what we heard, what we have heard since leaving. I have tried to put it all together, to come up with my own comprehensive reaction. Like so much in life, it is a mixture of good and evil, beauty and ugliness, kindness and cruelty.

Probably the overriding impression is of the damage China did to herself during the Cultural Revolution. It seems much more than the ten lost years that the Chinese kept telling us in 1977. This time we heard such horror stories it would have been impossible to believe them if we had not seen the scars and watched the tears fall. The son of a Tibetan whose parents were allowed to leave their country recently told me he could not take in what they told him. Tale after tale of hate, cruelty, revenge, torture, murder. A Chinese doctor who lives abroad said he felt his country had suffered a psychotic episode. A Tibetan said Tibet had been ravaged, words which were echoed by a Chinese about China.

Somehow the destruction in Tibet has left the worst

155

feeling in me. It was so organized, so arrogant, so wicked. We have been told that the Chinese sent trained delegations to strip the monasteries, to empty them of everything of value, jewels, gold, silver, art works. Then the Chinese army was sent in to destroy the buildings. After that, local Tibetans were told they could have the remains for firewood. If there are only two thousand monks left out of 120,000 what happened to the rest?

I have been told by a recent visitor that many Tibetans suffer from hypertension, from stress-related illnesses. I asked if they were not just upper-class people who had had a hard time, and the answer was no, many were former servants, which means serfs.

Where is it all heading? Sixty percent of the Chinese cadres will be leaving Tibet, if they have not left by now. The Chinese are interested only in foreign affairs and the military, they told us. Tibetans will be permitted, encouraged, to manage their other affairs, agriculture, animal husbandry and local government. They will be allowed to practice their religion if they so wish.

But will they be able to manage? Everything seemed in such a state of flux, of change! Which way will it settle? We had the feeling it would be a good thing for the Dalai Lama to return now while policy is still up in the air and undetermined, so he could influence the changes. Tibetans have told us they feel it is too early, he would be helpless in such a jumble. Will the many Tibetan refugees who have finally made a life for themselves in other places want to return to their country, which is so changed? Will the Tibetans who remained welcome them back? How can they get along with erstwhile serfs? How do they all feel about each other? Can they forget the past, stop the recriminations, work together to rebuild the country and the society?

The patient has been sick, has been given such harsh treatment he is sick from the treatment. To restore and rebuild his health will take an enormous effort by the Chinese and all the Tibetan groups, inside and outside Tibet. It can be done, but only with patience and good will.

Travel Tips

A visitor to China should realize that it is a very informal country. Very few changes of clothes are necessary. While Chinese women wear skirts more often than they used to, the usual way of dressing is still pants and a shirt. And they wear no jewelry, only a serviceable wristwatch.

Even knowing what I do and having been to China before, for this last visit, I took too much. For a six-week trip of rugged traveling in deserts and mountains, which also included a week in Beijing with dinners at restaurants and Chinese people's homes, the opera and other cultural events, several days in different large cities, days and nights on trains, trips in regular planes and cargo planes, drives in cars, buses and jeeps—the following is all I needed, and all I wore:

> two pairs of slacks, one khaki and one black (take two fullish, easy street-length skirts if you don't like pants)
>
> one reversible wrap-around skirt, black on one side, checked on the other
>
> three shirts or blouses to go with the above
>
> one dress for dinners in cities—mine was white-dotted navy voile, shirtwaist style, with long sleeves
>
> one pair of comfortable light walking shoes, like sneakers
>
> one pair of flat sandals
>
> shoes for travel that will double for evening (mine were sandals with heels)
>
> sweater and a windbreaker jacket, which I wore in

Tibet

underclothes, two nightgowns, wrapper, slippers and pantyhose and one pair of light wool socks, which I only wore to bed in Tibet.

For cold weather I would take the same things in heavier material, and a warm coat, cap, gloves, boots, scarf—what we wear at home in the northeast in winter.

Everything except shoes should be washable. I wash my clothes every night when traveling and they are dry in the morning. I take three plastic fold-up hangers and a stretchy line to hang things on in the bathroom. I wash Harrison's socks when we are to be in the same place for two nights. Hotel laundries are satisfactory and he sends everything else out.

Men can travel lightly, too. My suggestions are:

For summer:

two pairs of washable pants

one lightweight suit—can be drip dry

shirts and sport shirts—remember, the laundry comes back the same day

sneakers or fabric, rubber-soled shoes

two pairs of other shoes (sandals, if you like them)

sweater

underclothes, socks, pajamas

bathrobe and slippers

For winter:

two suits

two sweaters

warm weatherproof coat

hat or cap, scarf, gloves etc.

bathrobe, slippers, underclothes etc.

The main thing to remember is that often you may have to carry your own bag.

159

I haven't included a raincoat for warm weather because we never wore ours, as it was too hot. An umbrella is much better and you can buy one in China and use it in the hot sun. Now you can buy many things that were not available on both our previous trips. For instance, in the Beijing Hotel they sell a large variety of western liquor—scotch, gin, vodka, etc. At least they did in 1980. The China travel guidebook says you can buy western liquor in most big cities, but we found it only in Beijing. Also in Beijing, Max Factor and other cosmetics are available, and at the Chinese drug counter, absorbent cotton. But there are no tissues anywhere. Often one gets caught without toilet paper, so take along some small packages of tissues in your purse or pocket.

Hotels supply soap but no washcloths. These you can buy in the Beijing Hotel. But take all the film you think you will need. In Xi'an, a roll of 35 mm. film costs ten dollars.

I pack aspirin, an antibiotic and vitamin pills and any special cosmetic, but Chinese women don't wear makeup, so you don't need to either, if you don't want to. You won't look queer to anyone, except perhaps yourself.

All hotels and guest houses supply hot, boiled water in Thermos jugs so you can have tea or coffee any time you like. Generally there is tea in your room, but you may want to take your own instant coffee.

There are hairdressers and barbers in the hotels.

We always carry a short-wave radio. It is comforting to hear the BBC and the Voice of America when one is so far from home.

INDEX